Building Relationships That Last

Life's Bottom Line

by

RICHARD EXLEY

Tulsa, Oklahoma

Building Relationships That Last
— Life's Bottom Line
ISBN 0-89274-565-7
Copyright © 1990 by Richard Exley
7807 E. 76th St.
Tulsa, Oklahoma 74133-3678

Published by Honor Books
P. O. Box 55388
Tulsa, Oklahoma 74155-1388

DEDICATION

To Weldon and Elaine McMath, special friends for all seasons. They have been with us in the good times and the bad. Truly they are a gift from God.

Contents

ACKNOWLEDGMENTS

INTRODUCTION

Part I

GOD

1 JACOB AND OTHER ENTREPRENEURS — 31
2 JACOB'S SALVATION — 39
3 SIMON MAGNUS AND OTHER KINGDOM BUILDERS — 49
4 OVERCOMING THE SIMON MAGNUS SPIRIT — 59
5 REDEEMING YOUR DIFFICULTIES — 69
6 THE DIVINE TASK — 77
7 THE DIVINE DESIRE — 89
8 THE DIVINE GOAL — 97

Part II

INWARDNESS

9 THE INWARD JOURNEY — 113
10 THE KEY TO UNDERSTANDING YOURSELF — 125
11 FACING THE TRUTH ABOUT OURSELVES — 137
12 FREE AT LAST — 147

Part III

SIGNIFICANT OTHERS

13 THE DIVINE IDEAL — 161
14 MAKING THE DIVINE IDEAL REAL — 171

15 THE MEANING OF MARRIAGE — PART I   177
16 THE MEANING OF MARRIAGE — PART II   189
17 REMEMBERING OUR ROOTS   199
18 THE MAKING OF A FAMILY   209

Part IV

COMMUNITY

19 "AS IRON SHARPENS IRON"   233
20 SPECIAL FRIENDS   241
21 OWNING OUR MISTAKES   251
22 RESTORING BROKEN RELATIONSHIPS   261

ACKNOWLEDGMENTS

Having just reread the completed manuscript, I cannot help but realize how indebted I am to so many people, most of whom I have never met personally. I'm referring, of course, to all those writers whose efforts have shaped my thinking and enriched my life. I have conscientiously tried to give credit where credit is due; still I realize that all of "my" thoughts and insights are rooted in the things I have learned from others. The words may be my own, but the "truth" belongs to all of you. The benefits of this work then also belong to all of you, for without your contribution to my life I would have nothing to say. The shortcomings, however, are mine alone.

Special acknowledgment goes to Bruce Larson, Keith Miller and Robert Raines whose writings, years ago, introduced me to the theology of relationships. I am also indebted to Frederick Buechner, John Killinger, David Redding and Walter Wangerin, Jr. for their literary style, as well as their penetrating insights into the human dilemma and God's grace. Dr. James Dobson's books have shaped my understanding of marriage and the family. Charles Swindoll's conversational style of relating scriptural truths and his prodigious productivity never cease to challenge me. To each of you I express my deepest thanks.

There are scores of others, too numerous to name, but let me mention: William Barclay, Bob Benson, Anthony Campolo, John Claypool, Dr. Gary Collins, Charles Colson, Maxie Dunnam, Richard Foster, Arthur Gordon, Harold Kushner, Gordon MacDonald, Michel Quoist, David A. Seamands, R. C. Sproul, Dr. Paul Tournier and H. Norman Wright. You have been my teachers, and I will always be in your debt. There is no way I can repay you, but I do hope I can pass on to others something of what you have imparted to my life.

Building Relationships That Last

Life's Bottom Line

INTRODUCTION

Have you ever been lonely? I am not talking about the late-night melancholy so common to insomniacs, a melancholy that is dissipated with each new day. Nor am I referring to that vague loneliness that afflicts even the most gregarious from time to time. I mean, have you ever felt totally alone, as if there were no one who really knew you, no one with whom you could truly share your heart, your life?

When I think of that kind of loneliness, several memories come to mind like slides projected on a screen. Once, while reading *Living the Adventure* by Keith Miller, I found myself weeping, so completely could I identify with his loneliness.

"Last winter," he wrote, "I was sitting in a house at the beach, looking out the window and watching the driven gray rain blow the sea grass almost flat on the dunes. Alone in the house, I heard the wind howling, announcing the storm which was moving in from the Gulf. Ordinarily I would have felt an exciting surge of creativity and been inspired. But I was numb and simply stared blankly. I wasn't really numb. I could feel. My whole body ached and I had a sudden need to cry, to sob, but the tears would not come — too much training 'to be a man.'

"At first I didn't know what was the matter. I knew I hadn't been able to write anything for months and felt that maybe I was through as a writer. I had driven myself so compulsively and for so long as a speaker and conference leader that speaking and leading conferences had lost their meaning for me. I felt like a 'religious program' instead of an ordinary person. Although I still believed in God intellectually, I had pushed him away, and my prayers were sporadic and not very real. Something had gone very wrong. And as I looked at the future I couldn't see any meaning or purpose. I thought, 'I guess I've done my thing.' I felt very sad and old and something else much deeper.

"Then I recognized where I was: *in the desert of loneliness.*"[1] (emphasis mine)

I could read no further, so I put my finger between the pages and sat there with silent tears running down my cheeks. I was weeping for Keith Miller who couldn't weep for himself, and I was weeping for myself, for all the time I had longed for a special friend, longed to know and be known. And I was weeping for you, all of you — the lonely drinker seeking escape in a bottle, the single parent struggling against all odds to make a normal life for herself and her children, the handicapped person who is shunned because he is different.

A second memory now replaces the first and slowly comes into focus. Several years ago while serving as a pastor in Colorado, I received a telephone call from one of the funeral directors asking if I could conduct a service. He gave me the name of the deceased and explained that it would be a small service. The dead man had no family and had spent the last twenty years in the Yampa Valley Nursing Home.

Two days later, I stepped behind the pulpit to begin the service. The small chapel was empty, totally deserted, except for the funeral director and the body of the deceased. A solitary couple sat forlornly in the family room behind the sheer curtains. Later I learned that the woman was a distant cousin, the deceased's only known relative.

As I opened the scriptures and began to read, I suddenly had a picture of the man's life bereft of family and friends. A great sadness engulfed me. The thought of it was almost more than I could bear. No wife or children, no brothers or sisters, no church family, no friends or neighbors, not a solitary soul to mourn his death.

With an effort I finished the short service and returned to my office. I've long since forgotten the name of the deceased man, but I've never been able to escape the memory of that forlorn chapel or the lonely life it epitomized.

As real as that experience is, and, believe me, it is more real than most of us will ever know, we must be careful lest we mistakenly assume that loneliness is the particular plight of those who by fate or circumstance are cut off from the company of others. Nothing could be further from the truth. Some of the loneliest people I've ever known have been married and/or surrounded by lots of people.

For them loneliness is lying awake in the dead of night tormented by the regular breathing of their sleeping spouse:

If only he had time to hear the cry of her heart, to know her secret fears and share her tentative dreams. If only she weren't so exhausted at the day's end. If she could just stop caring for the children long enough to hear his concerns. Unfortunately, she's far too busy. Even when they do have a little time together, she seems preoccupied with concerns of her own.

Loneliness is a public person with no personal life — a man (or woman) who is constantly surrounded by people, but who has no one with whom he can share his heart. Thomas Merton wrote in *No Man Is An Island:* "Great priests, saints like the Cure' d'Ars, who had seen into the hidden depths of thousands of souls, have, nevertheless, remained men with few intimate friends. No one is more lonely than a priest who has a vast ministry. He is isolated in a terrible desert by the secrets of his fellow men."[2]

Loneliness is the gut-wrenching feeling you get when you are misunderstood or, worse yet, ignored. I've known moments like that, and I'm sure you have too. Moments when you've finally dared to risk sharing some deeply personal concern, only to discover, in mid-sentence, that you are not being heard. Perhaps you paused for a breath, or to search for just the right word, or to regain your courage, only to have your "friend" cut in and begin talking about something totally unrelated. The embarrassed humiliation that seemed to swallow you was just the forerunner of a paralyzing loneliness.

What am I trying to say? Simply this — loneliness is a universal human phenomenon. Sooner or later we all experience it. It may persist for a few minutes or for a lifetime. Henri J. M. Nouwen, author of *Reaching Out*, says, "Psychiatrists and clinical psychologists speak about it as the most frequently expressed complaint and the root not only of an increasing number of suicides but also of alcoholism, drug use, and a host of different psychosomatic symptoms...."[3]

Others describe loneliness as an "almost permanent condition for millions of Americans....knowing no limits of class, race, or age."[4] "The late Powell Davies of Washington, D.C. wrote, 'we are all lonely under the stars, all strangers and sojourners here on earth.'"[5]

Having said all of that, let me hasten to add that loneliness should not be viewed as a weakness or a character defect of any kind. Just as the body expresses its need for food through hunger, so the soul expresses its need for relationships through feelings of loneliness. In truth, relationships are to the soul what breath is to the body; without them we cannot truly experience life.

Noted author Walter Wangerin, Jr., declares: "Personal meaning and human value arise only in relationship. Solitude casts doubt on them. Identity, too, is discovered only in relationship. Lacking companions at the level of the soul, I finally cannot find my soul. It always takes another person to show myself to me. Alone I die....

"Listen: particular and loving relationships are more than merely 'good'; they are an essential quality of life. They affirm the individual's being. They assure him that he is. They both support him physically and define him spiritually. They give him a special place in the world, and they acknowledge the good purpose of his presence in that place. It is more than comfort we receive from other people: it is identity, so I know who I am. It is being itself, and the conviction of personal worth."[6]

According to Christian psychologist Craig Ellison, there are three types of loneliness: existential, emotional and social.[7] *Existential loneliness* refers to that sense of "aloneness" a person experiences when he is separated from God. Frequently it is accompanied by an almost overwhelming feeling of emptiness, as if life has absolutely no meaning or purpose. *Emotional loneliness* occurs when an individual is deprived of a psychologically intimate relationship with another person or persons. *Social loneliness* involves a lack of identification with one's peers. The person who is experiencing this type of loneliness longs for an extended family, a support group, who will accept and affirm him.

Existential loneliness can only be resolved through a relationship with God. Augustine said it for all of us when he prayed, "Thou has formed us for Thyself and our hearts are restless till they find rest in Thee." Regardless of how intimately we relate to another human being, that person can never satisfy our inherent need for fellowship with God. No matter how well accepted we are by our peers or how popular we become, this social achievement will never fill our need for intimacy with our Divine Creator. Fellowship with the Father is the only resolution for our spiritual loneliness.

Yet, by the same token, God refuses to resolve our emotional or social loneliness except as we develop meaningful relationships with others. Shortly after creation, before the fall of man, while God and Adam were sharing perfect fellowship as Friend with friend, God said: ". . .'It is not good for the man to be alone. I will make a helper suitable for him'" (Gen. 2:18).

If Adam needed another human being to be fully fulfilled under those perfect conditions, then it should not surprise us to discover that we, too, have an inherent need to be psychologically intimate with at least one other person. God Himself satisfies the heart's desire for spiritual fellowship, but we must build human relationships with "significant others" in order to escape our emotional loneliness.

A person's need for emotional closeness is generally met through a relationship with a spouse and/or special friend. In *Marriage As a Vocation,* David R. Mace writes: "We can somehow endure pain, provided we can grasp a loving hand and be supported by a familiar arm. We can live through failure if only one dear companion goes on believing in us. But what we cannot endure is the experience of being utterly alone, without anyone to love us or care about us."[8]

In addition to our need for fellowship with the Father and emotional closeness with at least one other person, we also need an extended family. We must have a peer group in which we are known and accepted. In his book, *Pastoral Care for Lay People*, Frank Wright says: "In a relatively affluent society, it is perhaps the frustrating of our 'belonging' needs, the unhappiness of our personal relationships, which causes more frustration than any other. . . . My experience tells me that the world is full of people desperate not to join, but to belong. . . .There is a great hunger for contact, belongingness, a need to overcome feelings of alienation and strangeness. . . ."[9]

Yet even as we experience this "hunger for contact, belongingness," we are tempted to draw back. Ralph Keyes, the author of *We, the Lonely People,* while agreeing that most of us want a sense of community with others, adds, "...there are three things which we want more — mobility, privacy, and convenience, 'which are the very sources of our lack of community.'"[10] Now add to our self-centeredness the depersonalizing influences of our technological age plus the fear of rejection, and it is not hard to see why we are so lonely.

Far from being a negative influence, however, loneliness is often a positive force in our lives. That is not to say that it is painless, but only that it is a primary factor in moving us out of our isolation into community. Its painfulness motivates us to reach out to others in ways we would never dare risk if there were any other options.

If we could find a way to ease our loneliness, a way to satisfy our belonging needs, apart from the risk and inconvenience of relationships, we would no doubt take it. Therefore God refuses to totally satisfy our belonging needs through a personal relationship with Himself alone. Without the pain of loneliness, few of us would ever pay the price for community. After all, it only takes two or three disappointing experiences to convince us that relationships are high-risk endeavors. Often we are willing to risk reaching out to another only because our loneliness has become insufferable.

An alcoholic described his feelings this way: "The besetting torture of my life has been a sense of being in the wrong and liable to punishment for it. I have tried many ways of dealing with this mental plague. I have tried bluster, proclaiming that I was not in the wrong at all, and wishful thinking, pretending the haunting feeling wasn't really there. I've tried stern repression, resolving not to let my mind dwell morbidly upon it. I've tried hard work, the pursuit of amusement and diversion, and God knows I've tried getting drunk. Regardless of my evasive maneuvers, there — when the chase was ended — it was, ready to pounce.

"It is hard for me to describe the terror that goes with this. I tense up and shorten my breath and feel scared. I go on the defensive at all points, fairly bristling like a mental porcupine, yet with an underlying deeply panicked sense that my defense is not going to be successful. It means ultimatums impossible to meet, ostracism and disgrace and an eternity of unfriendliness."[11]

One night this man could bear the pain of his loneliness no longer. In desperation he risked reaching out through openness and confession. Cutting through all the falsehood of his life, his real self emerged. He wrote: "The kindness of God and man made it possible for me to admit wrong. . . .Though the experience is grueling, the reward is a life lived fully and actively before God and man completely without fear."[12]

Perhaps the secret is to stop fighting our loneliness and embrace it. Perhaps we should make peace with our pain, make it an ally instead of an enemy. Existential loneliness can become solitude — a holy aloneness in which we at last discover our Creator and the fellowship He desires to share with us. Emotional loneliness can become a source of compassionate understanding, insight into the isolation of others. Having accepted our own need for in-depth relationships as legitimate, we can now reach out and embrace those who are not yet capable of acknowledging their own need. The isolation we have each experienced can become a shared intimacy.

Even our social loneliness, the feeling that we are on the outside looking in, can become an invitation to reach out and become part of an extended family. Instead of "busyness" we now acknowledge the gnawing ache for what it is — a hunger for contact, a need to belong. No longer are we intimidated by the gregariousness of others; rather, their camaraderie becomes our hope. It's a promise extended convincing us that we, too, can experience the joy of belonging.

As improbable as it may seem at this moment, you, too, can experience the relationships for which you so desperately long. Your loneliness can give way to community, your isolation can yield to intimacy, and your spiritual estrangement can be replaced by fellowship with the Father. In truth, against all odds you can find fellowship in an impersonal world.

Endnotes

[1] Keith Miller and Bruce Larson, *Living the Adventure* (Waco: Word Books, 1975), p. 13.

[2] Thomas Merton, *No Man Is an Island,* (New York: Harcourt, Brace and World, Inc. 1955), p. 12.

[3] Henri J. M. Nouwen, *Reaching Out* (Garden City: Doubleday, 1975), p. 15.

[4] Suzanne Gordon, *Lonely in America* (New York: Simon and Schuster, 1976), p. 15. Permission granted by Suzanne Gordon. Copyright © 1976 by Suzanne Gordon.

[5] Charles Hembree, *Pocket of Pebbles* (Grand Rapids: Baker Book House, 1969), p. 74.

[6] Walter Wangerin, Jr., *As For Me and My House* (Nashville: Thomas Nelson, 1987), p. 58.

[7] Craig W. Ellison, "Loneliness: A Social-Developmental Analysis," *Journal of Psychology and Theology,* 6:3-17, 1978.

[8] David R. Mace, *Marriage As a Vocation,* quoted in *Fun and Games in Marriage* by Dorothy T. Samuel (Waco: Word Books, 1973), p. 7.

[9] Frank Wright, *Pastoral Care for Lay People* (London: SCM Press LTD, 1982), pp. 14,15.

[10]Ralph Keyes, *We, the Lonely People* (New York: Harper & Row Publishers, Inc., 1973).

[11]Gordon C. Hunter, *When the Walls Come Tumblin' Down* (Waco: Word Books, 1970), p. 67.

[12]Ibid.

Part I

GOD

"Love self for self's sake
Love God for self's sake
Love God for God's sake
Love self for God's sake"[1]

— *Bernard of Clairvaux*

Part I

GOD

In my experience I have observed four basic ways in which believers relate to God. First, there are those, as Bernard observed, who "love God for self's sake." Those who love Him only for what they can get out of Him. They use God for their own ends. Like the prodigal in Luke 15, they pray, ". . .give me. . ." (v. 12). These believers are consumed with getting, and know little or nothing of true relationship. As a consequence, they are often lonely and unfulfilled in the deepest part of their being.

Then there are those who grow past the "give me" stage only to become obsessed with a passion to be used by God for "His" glory. They pray to be empowered, to be used. They are preoccupied with doing, and often they have great zeal but little wisdom and even less love. They pray to be used by God, when, if the absolute truth were known, not a few of them really want to use God to further their own "ministry." They, too, know little of real fellowship with the Father. They lead lives of spiritual loneliness in spite of their religious involvement.

The danger in this kind of "relationship" is twofold. Even if the practitioner is successful in doing great things for God, he is often unfulfilled within. On the other hand, if God doesn't "use" him in some special way, he may well become disillusioned or even apostate, as in the case of Antonio Salieri, an ambitious but mediocre 18th-century composer.

In the popular film, "Amadeus," we hear Salieri pray: "Lord, make me a great composer. Let me celebrate Your glory through music. *And be celebrated myself. Make me famous through the world, dear God, make me immortal.* After I die, let people speak my name forever with love for what I wrote. In return I will give You my chastity, my industry, my deep humility, my life." (emphasis mine)

Upon first hearing, this prayer may sound noble, even sacrificial. In truth, it is blatantly self-serving and spiritually deadly, as becomes obvious later on in the film when the pious Salieri realizes that he will never be as gifted as the rougish Wolfgang Mozart. He becomes insanely jealous of the young musical genius and plots to destroy him. God, to Salieri's way of thinking, has betrayed him. In a graphic scene depicting his apostasy, we see him take the crucifix from the wall of his room and place it in the fire.

The third stage of spiritual development is characterized by a growing desire to be like Christ. Those who have attained this level of spiritual maturity are interested in being and becoming, as well as doing. They long ". . . .to be conformed to the likeness of his (God's) Son. . ." (Rom. 8:29). Like the penitent prodigal, they now pray, ". . .make me. . ." (Luke 15:19), rather than, "give me," or even "use me."

The fourth and final level of relationship with God focuses on spiritual intimacy. Those who reach this level long to know God and be known by Him. They hunger for relationship, and thus they pray with the psalmist, "Search me, O God, and know my heart. . ." (Ps. 139:23). Like Paul the apostle, they long ". . .to know Christ and the power of his resurrection and the fellowship of. . .his sufferings. . ." (Phil. 3:10).

In truth, the fully mature believer incorporates all four dimensions in his relationship with God. He trusts God to meet his daily needs without majoring on the kind of demanding prayers that often characterized his initial relationship with the Father. Being and becoming are now of more importance to him than mere doing. Not because he is any less zealous. Quite to the contrary. He has come to realize that true ministry is an expression of who he is in Christ, rather than simply something he does. And more than anything, he wants to know God and be known by Him.

Perhaps A. W. Tozer expressed it best when he penned this prayer: "Heavenly Father: Let me see your glory, if it must be from the shelter of the cleft rock and from beneath the protection of your covering hand, whatever the cost to me in loss of friends or goods or length of days *let me know you as you are, that I may adore you as I should.* Through Jesus Christ our Lord. Amen."[2] (emphasis mine)

Endnotes

[1]John Killinger, *For God's Sake, Be Human* (Waco: Word Books, 1970), p. 47.

[2]A. W. Tozer, *The Knowledge of the Holy,* quoted in *Disciplines for the Inner Life* by Bob Benson and Michael W. Benson (Waco: Word Books, 1985), p. 3.

Chapter 1

JACOB AND OTHER ENTREPRENEURS

"Loving God for Self's Sake"

"We don't read the Bible," said Kierkegaard, the Danish theologian, "it reads us." And so it does, doesn't it? Reads us like an open book. With uncanny accuracy it lays bare our deepest and most real selves. The temptation story is no longer just the narrative of Adam's fall. Now it's my story, yours, for who among us hasn't succumbed to the temptation, to the egotistical ambition, to be like God. Or, to say it another way, who among us hasn't played God for a time? Isn't this what's at the root of all of our sins, all of our conflicts — this desperate desire to "do it our way"?

And it isn't just the story of Adam and Eve which reads us, which lays bare our deepest selves, but every Biblical story. The Old Testament is literally crammed with biographical accounts, all of which expose the true character of our human nature. To tell you the absolute truth, I see something of myself in each of them.

For instance: Jacob is a conniver, a manipulator. So am I. Moses succumbs to his temper. So do I. David is disobedient. I'm guilty again. Elijah falls prey to discouragement. Me too! On and on it goes.

The Living Bible says: "All these things happened to them as examples — *as object lessons to us* — ...they were written down so that we could read about them and *learn from them...*" (1 Cor. 10:11). J. B. Phillips renders this same passage, "Now these things which happened to our ancestors are *illustrations of the way in which God works...*." (emphasis mine)

Jacob is a classic example of a man who loved God for self's sake. He was a spiritual entrepreneur. His aspirations were commendable, but his motives and his methods left something to be desired. As Esau, his brother, said: "...'Isn't he rightly named Jacob? He has deceived me these two times: He took my birthright, and now he's taken my blessing!'..." (Gen. 27:36).

In Old Testament times a man's name was often representative of his character, and in Jacob's case it was certainly true.* Everything he did, until that fateful night when he wrestled with God on the muddy bank of the Jabbok, was rooted in trickery and deceit. Like most of us, he came by his nature honestly. Both his father, Isaac, and

---

*Literally the word *Jacob* means "he grasps the heel," but figuratively it means "he deceives."[1]

his grandfather, Abraham, had been known to "pull a fast one." And his mother, Rebekah, was actually the master-mind behind his cruelest hoax, the deception of his blind and aged father.

Jacob was not a bad person, just a self-centered one. To his way of thinking, every situation and every relationship could be turned to his advantage. Nor did he have to look for ways to take advantage of people, they came looking for him. Like the time his brother, Esau, returned from hunting, absolutely famished.

"He said to Jacob, 'Quick, let me have some of that red stew!'. . . .

"Jacob replied, 'First sell me your birthright.'

" 'Look, I am about to die,' Esau said. 'What good is the birthright to me?'

"But Jacob said, 'Swear to me first.' So he swore an oath to him, selling his birthright to Jacob.

"Then Jacob gave Esau some bread and some lentil stew. . . ."

Genesis 25:30-34

It could be argued that what Jacob did was simply "good business." In his defense, it has been said that Esau didn't have to sell, no one forced him. Still, no righteous man can feel quite right about taking advantage of another's vulnerability.

Jacob's next ruse was an inexcusable, outright deception, and it enabled him to steal the blessing which was rightly his brother's. Following his mother's counsel, he dressed in Esau's clothes and covered his hands and the smooth part of his neck with goatskins so they would feel hairy like his brother's. The trick worked only too well. After poor, blind Isaac had eaten the meal prepared for him by Rebekah, he blessed Jacob thinking he was Esau. Hardly had the conniving Jacob made his exit before Esau came in to receive his father's blessing, only to discover, too late, that he had been duped again. "...Then Esau wept aloud" (Gen. 27:38).

This second scheme is indefensible. No rearrangement of the facts can make it into a hard-nosed business deal. It is outright trickery, deception of the most odious kind. Soon Esau's tearful remorse gave way to anger, then bitterness, and finally to a burning desire for revenge. "...'The days of mourning for my father are near;'" he said to himself, "'then I will kill my brother Jacob'" (Gen. 27:41).

When Jacob discovered his brother's bloody intentions, he fled for his life. Yet it was not just Esau's murderous rage he sought to escape, but the terrible truth of what he had become. He could not look into his father's blind eyes without seeing a reflection of his deceitful self. Nor could he bear his betrayed brother's brooding anger without being constantly reminded of his loathsome deed. Even his mother's doting presence was somehow condemning, for in her, his partner in deceit, he saw an unflattering reflection of himself.

Now this is where the story takes its most unusual turn, where we see God's grace at its best. Evening found Jacob exhausted and a long way from his destination. Tired from his hurried flight, he arranged some stones for a pillow and prepared to spend the night, alone, in the wilderness.

Almost instantly he fell into a deep sleep and had a dream, not the tormented nightmare of a fugitive, but a holy vision. In it he saw a ladder stretching between heaven and earth on which the angels of God were ascending and descending. God Himself was part of that dream, too. In it He spoke to Jacob personally, promising to bless and protect him.

At first reading this seems to be an outrageous miscarriage of justice. If ever there was a man who did not deserve the blessings of God, it was this conniving rascal. Yet, it is this very outrage that becomes our best hope. If God met Jacob in the midst of his sin, might not He come to us as well?

And for just a moment it seems that even the self-serving Jacob might be undone, might be transformed, by God's terrifying nearness. "When Jacob awoke from his sleep, he thought, 'Surely the LORD is in this place, and I was not aware of it.' He was afraid and said, 'How awesome is this place! This is none other than the house of God. . .'" (Gen. 28:16,17).

But that transformation suffered an untimely end. Soon Jacob's awe gave way to his old self-serving nature and he attempted to strike a bargain with the Almighty. "Then Jacob made a vow, saying, 'If God will be with me and will watch over me on this journey I am taking and will give me food to eat and clothes to wear so that I return safely to my father's house, then the LORD will be my God'" (Gen. 28:20,21).

That's not how it's supposed to be done, but, at least, it was a beginning. Jacob opened the door to his conniving heart, just a little, just enough to strike a bargain with God. And if that is the only foothold God can get in our selfish lives, He will allow us to "use" Him for a time, believing that in the end His persistent presence will overcome us. It took more than twenty years, but Jacob finally succumbed, finally became God's person.

This kind of relationship is self-serving, a kind of "loving God for self's sake," barely a step above the mass of humanity who "love self for self's sake." Still, it's a beginning, and sometimes that's the best we can manage. In truth, many believers have simply transferred their selfishness from the kingdom of darkness into the Kingdom of God. They "serve" God for what they can get out of it — forgiveness of sins, financial prosperity, perpetual health and unending happiness.

Most of us probably came to God for those very reasons, or ones very similar. Perhaps life had gotten out of hand — our marriage wasn't working out, one of our teenage children had gotten into drugs, we had found ourselves suddenly unemployed, or maybe it was a serious illness. In desperation we turned to God. Somewhere we remembered having heard the testimony of someone whose marriage had been saved after he had come to God. "Perhaps, it will work for me," we can remember thinking. "At least it's worth a try."

And so we came to God as a kind of last hope. Like Jacob, we bargained with Him. "God, if You will restore my marriage and bless my business, I will serve You for the rest of my life." It's more than we deserve, more than we have any right to expect, but still God meets us there, in our need. Soon things began to turn around and we became firm believers in the God Who does things for us.

The tragedy in all of this is that many believers never grow beyond the bargain they struck with God in the beginning. For them He is a kind of cosmic Santa Claus Whose only reason for being is to provide for their every whim. The emphasis in their relationship, if it can be called a relationship, is on getting.

This is a sensitive matter and I want to be careful how I deal with it. In no way do I wish to minimize the supernatural ways God intervenes in our natural lives. Yet neither am I willing to allow the spiritual life to become nothing more than a self-serving "faith," a means whereby we enhance the materialistic trappings of our lives. I will readily acknowledge that the Scriptures repeatedly affirm God's commitment to provide for all of our needs. Jesus Himself taught us to pray, " 'Give us each day our daily bread' " (Luke 11:3). Yet, in the totality of the spiritual life, these material blessings are nothing more than a consequence of the Father's loving faithfulness. And they must always remain a consequence. They must never become the focus of our relationship with God, let alone the goal!

Perhaps Jesus said it best: " '*And do not set your heart on what you will eat or drink; do not worry about it.* For the pagan world runs after all such things, and your Father knows that you need them. *But seek his kingdom*, and these things will be given to you as well' " (Luke 12:29-31). (emphasis mine)

God wills to provide for all of our needs, but material blessing and marital bliss are not His highest concerns. Our world view is temporal; God's is eternal. We worry about daily concerns such as career goals, success and personal security, while He concerns Himself with our character.

With eternal wisdom He reasons, "'What good will it be for a man if he gains the whole world, yet forfeits his soul?...'" (Matt. 16:26). In short, God is determined to make us not just happy, but holy.

Endnotes

[1]Footnote on Genesis 27:36 in *The Holy Bible, New International Version* (Grand Rapids: Zondervan Bible Publishers, 1973, 1978, 1984).

Chapter 2

JACOB'S SALVATION
"Loving God for God's Sake"

From that very moment, at Bethel, when Jacob opened his heart just a crack, God began to work on him. At first it was nothing more than bringing him face to face with himself. Soon this schemer met one who was more than his match. Or in the words of Alexander Whyte, an English expositor of extraordinary gifts:

". . .he is cheated out of his wages, and cheated out of his wife and cheated, and cheated, and cheated again, ten times cheated, and that too by his own mother's brother, till cheating came out of his nostrils, and stank in his eyes, and became as hateful as hell to his heart.

"We say that Greek sometimes meets Greek. We say that diamond sometimes cuts diamond. . . .We speak about

the seller being sold. And we quote David to the effect that
to the froward God will show himself froward; and Paul
to the same effect, that as a man soweth so shall he reap.
Yes. Other people had been cheating their fathers and their
brothers all these years as well as Rebekah and Jacob. Other
little boys had been taking prizes in the devil's sly school
besides Rebekah's favorite son. Laban, Rebekah's brother,
and bone of her bone, had been making as pious speeches
at Bethuel's blind bedside as ever Jacob made at Isaac's.
And now that the actors are all ready, and the stage is all
built, and the scenery is all hung up, all the world is invited
in to see the seriocomedy of the Syrian bitter bit, or
Rebekah's poor lost sheep shorn to the bone by the steely
shears of Shylock her brother.

" 'What is this that thou hast done unto me? Wherefore
hast thou so beguiled me?' — Jacob appeared and
remonstrated in his sweet, injured, salad innocence.

"Jacob had never seen or heard the like of it in his
country. It shocked terribly and irrecoverably Jacob's inborn
sense of right and wrong; it almost shook down Jacob's
whole faith in the God of Bethel. And so still. We never
see what wickedness there is in lies, and treachery, and
cheatery, and injury of all kinds till we are cheated and lied
against, and injured ourselves. We will sit all our days and
speak against our brother till some one comes and reports
to us what they say who sit and speak against us. And then
the whole blackness and utter abominableness of detraction
and calumny and slander breaks out upon us, till we cut
out our tongue rather than ever again so employ it.

"It was Jacob's salvation that he fell into the hands
of that cruel land-shark, his uncle Laban. Jacob's salvation
is somewhat nearer now than when he believed at Bethel;

but, all the same, what is bred in the bone is not got clean rid of in a day."[1]

Seldom do the Jacobs of this world change until they begin to reap the consequences of their selfish nature. Only when they find the tables turned, only when they look their betrayer in the eyes and see themselves, do they begin to realize just how wretched they have become. In truth, "It was Jacob's salvation that he fell into the hands of that cruel land-shark, his uncle Laban."

Think for a moment. Don't we despise in others the very weakness and wickedness that we can't overcome in ourselves? When we succumb to some cruel and selfish temptation, we rationalize it away. But when we see it in another, we call it for what it really is — sin! And it is a blessed and terrible moment when, at last, we realize that what we despise in others is nothing less than the monster within ourselves. It is a blessed moment because having finally faced the truth, we can begin to deal with it. And yet it is a terrible moment too, painful and terrifying, for who can bear to look upon his own wretchedness?

When a person is converted, he seldom realizes the depth of his sinfulness. He confesses his "sins" (that is, those things he has done) and seeks the forgiveness of God. But it is not until later, often much later, that he begins to realize that the real sin is not something he has done, but something he is. Then, like Augustine, he cries: "O Lord. You took me from behind my own back, where I had placed myself because I did not wish to look upon myself. You stood me face to face with myself so that I might see how foul I am, how deformed and defiled, how covered with stains and sores. I looked and was filled with horror, but there was no place for me to flee to get away from myself."[2]

Such self-knowledge is painfully devastating. I mean, who can bear to be brought face to face with the evil within? Who can look upon his own unmitigated rapaciousness and not be undone? And yet this distressing truth is also the beginning of our salvation.

It took all of twenty years, and a thinly disguised family feud of long standing, to finally bring Jacob to his moment of truth. So bitter had become his plight that he decided he would rather return home and face Esau's wrath than spend another day enduring the thinly disguised resentment of his brothers-in-law. They hated him and mounted a whisper campaign among themselves: ". . . 'Jacob has taken everything our father owned and has gained all this wealth from what belonged to our father' " (Gen. 31:1).

As a result, ". . . Jacob noticed that Laban's attitude toward him was not what it had been" (Gen. 31:2). "So he fled with all he had, and crossing the River, he headed for the hill country of Gilead" (Gen. 31:21).

The only real difference between this journey and the one he took twenty years earlier is the fact that this time he isn't alone. He is accompanied by his wives and children, as well as his servants and livestock. Still, he is fleeing again. And this time he has no place to go. He has escaped the pursuing Laban only to be confronted by the prospect of facing Esau after all these years.

As is often the case, his desperate situation drives him to prayer. ". . . O God . . . , I am unworthy of all the kindness and faithfulness you have shown your servant. . . . Save me, I pray, from the hand of my brother Esau, for I am afraid he will come and attack me, and also the mothers with their children" (Gen. 32:9-11).

In desperation he divides his party into two groups and sends them out in different directions, hoping that at least one band may escape Esau's wrath. After they have disappeared into the dark, he finds himself alone. Only he isn't alone. His past returns to haunt him. After all these years, and all his successes, he still cannot escape the despicable things he has done. And he knows that it is not just something he did, not just a deed separate and apart from himself. Rather it was and is an extension of his very self. He and the deed are one! The thing he cannot escape, the thing he can no longer bear, is himself.

Now his lies and deceptions leer at him from the gloom. He sees again Esau's anger, hears him vow to kill him, tastes anew his youthful fear. Through trembling lips he murmurs, "...O God....Deliver me, I pray thee, (deliver me)..." (Gen. 32:9,11 KJV).

Then he turns to an old habit, a thing he has used across the years when the memories have come, biting and bitter. He begins to rationalize, to justify his deceitfulness. Hadn't Esau willingly sold his birthright? Wasn't it Rebekah, his own mother, who helped him dupe his poor, blind father? Helped nothing! It was her idea; without her insistence he would have called the whole thing off.

It sounded good. He almost convinced himself, but he knew his own heart too well. He knew that with or without his mother's help he would have stolen Esau's blessing. "Jacob is my rightful name," he mutters almost inaudibly. "I am a deceiver."

In his *Confessions,* Augustine relates the story of a youthful escapade in which he and some friends stole pears from a neighbor's tree. "We took great loads of fruit from it," he says, "not for our own eating but rather to throw it to the pigs."[3] The thing that made this act so loathsome to Augustine was the fact that it served no purpose other than as an expression of his sinful self. More than any other single act, it revealed his true depravity. "The fruit I gathered," he wrote, "I threw away, devouring in it only iniquity. There was no other reason, but foul was the evil and I loved it."[4]

It's terribly painful to admit that the problem is us. It's not circumstances, not temperament, not personality, not even the evil thing we have done, but us! Painful? Yes. But it is also good to have called it by its rightful name — sin — because having fearlessly owned our own sinfulness, we can now be forgiven and changed.

Let's return for a moment to Jacob, alone on the muddy bank of the Jabbok, for in his experience we have a graphic depiction of our own soul's terrible struggle. It is never easy to "name" ourselves, to admit that we are not the persons we have pretended to be. In fact, even after circumstances have made further denial not only futile but foolish, we are still tempted to protest our innocence and to rationalize our behavior. Like Jacob, we, too, wrestle with God, attempting to wrest a blessing from Him, rather than casting ourselves on His mercy.

See Jacob as he huddles in the dark, tormented by a host of unholy memories. A twig snaps, and instantly he is fully alert, sensing danger. He listens intently, hardly breathing, but hears only the small night sounds. After a bit, his heart resumes its normal rhythm, and he relaxes. When he does, his unseen adversary is upon him. Had murder been his assailant's intent, Jacob would have been a dead man, but as it is they thrash about on the muddy bank, each seeking an advantage.

If ever there was a man who deserved the judgments of God, it was conniving, deceitful Jacob. Yet it is precisely at this moment, when the conniver and deceiver seems about to reap the consequences of his lifelong deceitfulness, that God chooses to manifest His goodness. A goodness, pure and holy, like a terrible light penetrating to the deepest and darkest corners of his soul. And in that blessed agony, Jacob sees himself as he really is. God's holy light has stripped him of all pretentiousness. In deepest humility, he confesses: "My name is Jacob. All my life I've been a liar and a deceiver. I've used people. I've even used You; at least, I've tried."

Such a confession enables us, as Wangerin says, to "...take some control over it (that is, 'us' — our recalcitrant selves)." He goes on to say, "When you are required to speak the thing aloud, in all its facts...you can no longer deceive yourself or skip significant, spiritual details. Speaking it aloud in accurate words finally eliminates the lie — at least this once....Confessing the deed means calling it a sin, your sin, your own fault."[5]

Now comes the most wonderful part of this ancient story — Jacob is changed! He is not simply forgiven, but changed. God says that he is no longer Jacob, but Israel; no longer a self-serving entrepreneur, but a prince. He no longer loves God simply for self's sake, for what he can get out it. Now he loves God for God's sake, because God is truly worthy to be worshipped and loved.

Jacob is still not a perfect man (no one is, not in this life), but he is changed! The self-centered youth who bargained with God at Bethel has now become Israel, a prince. Instead of praying, ". . .'If. . .(You) will be with me and will watch over me on this journey I am taking and will give me food to eat and clothes to wear so that I return safely to my father's house, then. . .(You) will be my God'" (Gen. 28:20,21), he now prays, "'I am unworthy of all the kindness and faithfulness you have shown your servant. . .'" (Gen. 32:10). And, as unbelievable as it may seem, limping Israel has a power with God and men that the self-reliant Jacob never had.

"So Jacob called the place Peniel, saying, 'It is because I saw God face to face, and yet my life was spared'" (Gen. 32:30).

What Jacob experienced that night, in the dark, on the muddy bank of the Jabbok, was true prayer — life-changing prayer! We used to have prayer meetings like that. "Praying through," we called it, which meant we weren't leaving the place of prayer until God had touched us, cleansed us, made us new! There's an element of truth, a vital element, in the popular teaching on prayer which says to ask, believe, and receive, to "confess and possess." But if we ever forget the widow's importunity (Luke 18), or the empty-handed host's midnight persistence (Luke 11), or Jacob's stubborn determination (Gen. 32), we will have lost an irreplaceable part of our birthright. ". . .The effectual fervent prayer of a righteous man (still) availeth much" (James 5:16 KJV).

Jacob's lonely prayer vigil reminds me of something Emilie Griffin wrote in *Clinging — The Experience of Prayer:*

"Prayer is, after all, a very dangerous business. For all the benefits it offers of growing closer to God, it carries with it one great element of risk: the possibility of change. *In prayer we open ourselves to the chance that God will do something with us that we had not intended.* We yield to possibilities of intense perception, of seeing through human masks and the density of 'things' to the very center of reality. This possibility excites us, but at the same time there is a fluttering in the stomach that goes with any dangerous adventure. We foresee a confrontation with the unknown, being hurt, being frightened, being chased down.

"Don't we know for a fact that people who begin by 'just praying' — with no particular aim in mind — wind up trudging off to missionary lands, entering monasteries, taking part in demonstrations, dedicating themselves to the poor and the sick?...Isn't this what holds us back — the knowledge of God's omnipotence, his unguessability, his power, his right to ask all of us, a perfect gift of self, a perfect act of full surrender?"[6]

Yet, finally, isn't this what also brings us to "see God face to face," the knowledge of His omnipotence, His "unguessability," His power, His right to ask all of us, His ability to ultimately deliver us from our selfish selves, to make us new in every way?

Endnotes

[1]Alexander Whyte, D.D., *Bible Characters* (Grand Rapids: Zondervan Publishing House, 1967), p. 113.

[2]Charles W. Colson, *Loving God* (Grand Rapids: A Judith Markham Book, Zondervan Publishing House, 1983), p. 49.

[3]*The Confessions of St. Augustine,* translated by John K. Ryan (New York: Doubleday, 1960), pp. 69-72.

[4]Ibid.

[5]Walter Wangerin, Jr., *As For Me and My House* (Nashville: Thomas Nelson, 1987), p. 201.

[6]Emilie Griffin, *Clinging — The Experience of Prayer,* quoted in *Disciplines for the Inner Life* by Bob Benson and Michael W. Benson (Waco: Word Books, 1985), pp. 232,233.

Chapter 3

SIMON MAGNUS AND OTHER KINGDOM BUILDERS

"Loving God for Self's Sake"

Inbred in fallen humanity are two burning desires — a love for money and a quest for power. At one time Christianity confronted these issues, identified them for the evil they are, and challenged men and women to renounce them and give their allegiance only to Jesus Christ. Unfortunately, in this age of affluence the pursuit of prosperity and power has been once again falsely legitimized. Or as Paul Tournier notes, ". . .the GNP is the modern Golden Calf."[1]

Instead of challenging this crass materialism, in some cases ministers have actually appealed to these baser desires.

They have, in fact, promised wealth and power to those who will follow Christ.

What makes this such a difficult issue to address is the fact that God does promise both to bless and to empower His people. However, at least two things distinguish His blessing from the power-brokering materialism of the world. First, it is a consequence, rather than a goal. Spiritually mature believers seek only the Kingdom of God. These other things (i.e., wealth and power) are truly unsought. To mature Christians, they are merely an expression of their Father's goodness, not a personal goal to be attained. Second, they see themselves as stewards of these things, not owners. All wealth and power belong to the Father. They are simply managing them (that is, using them for the good of His Kingdom).

Neither wealth nor power is inherently evil. Dangerous, to be sure, but not evil. It is the inordinate desire for these things that is immoral. Or as Paul says, "...the love of money is a root of all kinds of evil..." (1 Tim. 6:10).

When a person is converted to Christ, these inherent evils are defeated in his life, but not destroyed (that is, they have lost their stranglehold on his human will, but they have not been totally eradicated). Once these things reigned on the throne of our lives, controlling us. Now they huddle in the far corners of our consciousness. They are powerless until we voluntarily yield to their control, then they become our obsessive masters.

No truly spiritual person would knowingly embrace them, and yet many have succumbed to their mesmerizing power. The Apostle Paul writes, "...Some people, eager for money, have wandered from the faith and pierced themselves with many griefs" (1 Tim. 6:10). According to the Scriptures, these temptations often come disguised as spiritual gifts or blessings, a kind of divine right. Paul describes those who fall prey to this deception as ". . .men of corrupt mind, who have been robbed of the truth and *who think that godliness is a means to financial gain*" (1 Tim. 6:5). (emphasis mine)

Richard Foster writes in *Money, Sex & Power:* ". . .we defeat the powers by forthrightly facing the 'demons' within. Right at the outset, we all need to see and to address the powers that nip at our own heels. . . .We must look squarely in the face of our greed and lust for power and see them for what they are. We must look at ourselves spiritually and discern ourselves spiritually.

"The glory is that we do not do this alone. The blessed Holy Spirit comes alongside of us and comforts and encourages as he convicts and reproves. He leads us into the inner solitude of the heart where he can speak to us and teach us. . . .In this interior silence we hear the *Kol Yahweh*, the voice of the Lord. Hearing, we turn from our violence, our greed, our fear, our hate. Hearing, we turn to Christ's love and compassion and peace."[2]

In Chapter 2, we saw how Jacob finally heard the voice of God and truly turned to Him. As a result, he was able to overcome his greedy materialism and has become an example of God's grace for all of us who long to grow beyond simply "loving God for self's sake."

Unfortunately, the love of money is only one of the ways this aberration manifests itself. Now we turn our attention to the second — a lust for power. Not the kind of lust found in the unmitigated ambition of the world's powermongers, but rather that which disguises itself in the trappings of spirituality. The kind of yearning for power that is half-holy and half-profane. The kind that plagues zealous men and women of God.

For years I served as pastor of small churches in rural areas, yet I struggled with this lust for power. "Like the twelve, I wanted to be the greatest in the kingdom, and I wanted all the 'perks' that came with it. I justified my ambition by interpreting it as a vision for the kingdom, a divine call for my life, God's will, and herein lies part of the deception. I was committed to the kingdom, I did care about reaching the world with the Gospel, but it was all tangled up with my own ego needs.

"As disconcerting as it may be, the fact is that ambition and obedience will probably always share the seat of power in the minister's life. It's not ideal, but it is, I think, a realistic appraisal of the minister and the ministry. Our salvation does not come in totally divorcing ourselves from personal ambition, that's virtually impossible, but in recognizing it for what it is and honestly dealing with it. The real trouble starts when we experience success and interpret that as divine approval for all of our motives. When that happens there's little or nothing left to restrain our ambitious egos."[3]

Some people lust after power because they simply cannot bear to live outside of the limelight. Simon Magnus, the sorcerer of Samaria, was such a man. Luke tells us that "...for some time a man named Simon had practiced sorcery in the city and amazed all the people of Samaria. He boasted that he was someone great, and all the people, both high and low, gave him their attention and exclaimed,

'This man is the divine power known as the Great Power.' They followed him because he had amazed them for a long time with his magic" (Acts 8:9-11).

Then Philip the evangelist came to town, and everything changed:

"When the crowds heard Philip and saw the miraculous signs he did, they all paid close attention to what he said. With shrieks, evil spirits came out of many, and many paralytics and cripples were healed. So there was great joy in that city.

". . .when they believed Philip as he preached the good news of the kingdom of God and the name of Jesus Christ, they were baptized, both men and women."

Acts 8:6-8,12

Then "Simon himself believed and was baptized. And he followed Philip everywhere, astonished by the great signs and miracles he saw" (Acts 8:13).

It is not our place to challenge the validity of Simon's conversion; still, one cannot help but question his motives, especially in light of his proposal to Peter and John. Luke writes, "When Simon saw that the Spirit was given at the laying on of the apostles' hands, he offered them money and said, 'Give me also this ability so that everyone on whom I lay my hands may receive the Holy Spirit'" (Acts 8:18,19).

It would appear that Simon Magnus, if he truly loved God at all, loved Him only for self's sake. He was a discerning man and obviously realized that with the manifestation of the Holy Spirit's power his old magic was of little consequence. The attention the Samaritans had once heaped upon him, they now lavished on Philip and the apostles.

Alexander Whyte writes: "Now, Simon Magus, like everybody else in Samaria, was immensely impressed with all that he saw and heard. No man was more impressed than Simon Magus, or more convinced of the divine mission of the apostles. But, with all his wonder and with all his conviction, he was never truly converted. The love of money, *and the still more intoxicating love of notoriety* had taken such absolute possession of Simon Magus that he simply could not live out of the eyes of men. He must be in men's mouths. He must have a crowd around him."[4] (emphasis mine)

It's sad to say, but there is undoubtedly something of Simon Magnus in even the best of us. A certain need for public attention. Possibly it is less crass than the unmitigated variety manifested by that self-serving sorcerer, but it's there nonetheless. Frequently it motivates us to ". . .eagerly desire spiritual gifts. . ." (1 Cor. 14:1), but for the wrong reasons. Our primary goal is not ministry, but popularity; not God's glory, but our own.

Jim Gilbert, a songwriter and satirist, cuts to the very core of our mixed motives when he writes:

"What would you do Lord
Without all your superstars?
With us as your sponsors
You just might go pretty far
You need our endorsement
That's why we go in your name
You need the souls we save
And we need the fame. . . .

"I'll be your superstar
I'll tell them who you are
I'll put your name right there
In lights beneath my own. . . .

"Nearly three billion people
All still waiting to hear
I could build up your kingdom
If you'd boost my career
And I long to tell them, Lord,
How you suffered and bled
For thirty-five hundred a night
Plus my overhead"[5]

If this lust for "spiritual" power is not dealt with quickly, it will ruin the man or woman of God. Initially it simply creates confusion in the Body of Christ. Taken to its ultimate conclusion, however, it produces charlatans and false prophets, wolves in sheep's clothing. "They are the kind who worm their way into homes and gain control over weak-willed women, who are loaded down with sins and are swayed by all kinds of evil desires" (2 Tim. 3:6).

"In his brilliant book, *Nicholas and Alexandra*, Robert K. Massie tells how the Tsar and Empress of Russia were misled by a miracle and thus brought their great empire down to dust.

"After many years of anxious waiting for an heir to the Russian throne, Tsar Nicholas II and his German wife, Federovna, were blessed with a son. However, their hopes for the future were cruelly crushed six weeks later when doctors discovered the infant had hemophilia, an incurable blood disease that could kill at any moment. All of his short life was to be lived in the shadow of terror, with death stalking every footstep. This tragedy introduced into the royal family one of the most evil men who ever lived.

"Several times the young tsarevich slipped close to death. Seeing him writhe in excruciating pain, his tormented parents would beg doctors to do something, but they were helpless. In those moments they turned to Gregory Rasputin, a religious mystic of questionable credentials, later known as the mad monk of Russia. Invariably, he would pray for the boy and there would be a marked improvement. Even today doctors are at a loss to explain how these healings took place, but history testifies to them. Always, Rasputin would warn the parents the boy would only live as long as they listened to him.

"Rasputin's power over the royal family became so great he could, with a word, obtain the appointment or dismissal of any government official. He had men appointed or dismissed on the basis of their attitudes toward himself rather than their abilities. Consequently, the whole Russian government reeled under the unwise counsel of this evil man. Seeds of revolution were planted and watered with discontent. It erupted into the murder of the royal family, internal war, and the communistic takeover. Alexander Kerensky, a key government figure during those trying times, later reflected, 'Without Rasputin, there could have been no Lenin.' "[6]

Thankfully, the New Testament Church was spared such a tragedy when Peter discerned the true intent of Simon's heart and addressed it forthrightly. ". . .'May your money perish with you,'" he said, " 'because you thought you could buy the gift of God with money! You have no part or share in this ministry, *because your heart is not right before God.* Repent of this wickedness and pray to the Lord.

Perhaps he will forgive you for having such a thought in your heart. *For I see that you are full of bitterness and captive to sin'"* (Acts 8:20-23). (emphasis mine)

The Simons and Rasputins of the world are graphic examples of the abuse of spiritual power taken to its ultimate conclusion. Yet as tragic and dramatic as they are, they are not my primary concern. By the time a man or woman reaches this point, he or she is almost always totally deceived.

Writing in *The Communicator's Commentary on Acts,* Lloyd Ogilvie, Senior Pastor of Hollywood's First Presbyterian Church, says: "Peter used a very potent word in confronting Simon with his spiritual imperiousness and desire to get and control the Spirit — 'wickedness,' *poneria* in Greek, means compulsive determination to continue in a direction we know is wrong. It is sin which becomes so much the focus of the will that we no longer desire to change it and want God to approve it and bless us anyway. . . .This is pointedly exemplified in Simon's response to Peter. He completely sidestepped the challenge to repent. He asked Peter to pray that none of the things with which he confronted him would happen, but he did not do the one thing which could prevent it — repent! Simon was still in charge of Simon. . . ."[7]

My deepest concern, therefore, is not for the Simons of this world, but for those sincere, howbeit over-zealous, men and women who have allowed their desire to be "used" by God to become supplanted by personal ambition. Not infrequently such "spiritually" ambitious people accomplish magnificent things for God. And, as a result, they become known as great men and women of God. Unfortunately, when a person "loves God for self's sake" (that is, for what he can get out of it, i.e. recognition, personal acclaim and all that goes with it), he almost always ends up empty on the inside. The applause of men may be temporarily intoxicating, but it can never satisfy the soul's deepest hungers. Only fellowship with God can do that!

Endnotes

[1]Paul Tournier, *The Violence Within,* translated by Edwin Hudson (San Francisco: Harper & Row Publishers, Inc., 1978), p. 119.

[2]Richard Foster, *Money, Sex & Power* (San Francisco: Harper & Row Publishers, Inc., 1985), pp. 190,191.

[3]Richard Exley, *Perils of Power* (Tulsa: Honor Books, 1988), p. 76.

[4]Alexander Whyte, D.D., *Bible Characters* (Grand Rapids: Zondervan Publishing House, 1967), p. 121.

[5]Jim Gilbert, *Superstar* (Tulsa: Spirit & Soul Publishing Co., ASCAP, 1982).

[6]Charles Hembree, *Pocket of Pebbles* (Grand Rapids: Baker Book House, 1969), p. 11.

[7]Lloyd J. Ogilvie, *The Communicator's Commentary, Volume V: Acts* (Waco: Word Books, 1983), p. 158.

Chapter 4

OVERCOMING THE SIMON MAGNUS SPIRIT

I don't suppose any of us will ever be completely free of the personal ambition which taints our holiest desire to be used by God. Indeed, if absolutely pure motives were a prerequisite for service in the Kingdom, we would all be disqualified. Still, spiritual integrity demands that we constantly search our hearts before God and honestly confess our shortcomings. Only as we practice this holy discipline can we be assured of keeping our ambition in check.

Just a few weeks ago I had an opportunity to confront my own ambition again, and in an area in which I thought I had conquered it. After several days of painful discontentment, I was finally able to come to grips with my inner ambiguity, and I wrote in my journal:

"I felt a mandate from God to write *Perils of Power,* and I truly expected an overwhelming response. I feared that I might be attacked because of what I had written, that I might find myself in the midst of a controversy. Nothing yet, thank God! On the other hand, I felt that it would be a runaway best-seller. Not so, not even close! Reason tells me two months is hardly enough time to draw any real conclusions, but in my 'guts' I've been really disappointed.

"What does this disappointment say about me?"

"1) It says that pure ministry motives have been compromised by personal ambition. It lays bare my secret desire to be recognized as a best-selling author. *God help me*!

"2) It says that I'm feeling pressured to 'make' something happen.

How quickly we forget. The only good things that have ever happened in my ministry have been orchestrated by God apart from any ambitious manipulating on my part.

"3) It says that I'm looking to my writing for my financial security, rather than simply trusting in the Father's faithfulness. *Forgive me, O God*!

"Yesterday, after I had finally confronted this painful truth, I opened the Scriptures for my regular devotional reading and turned to the day's psalm which happened to be Psalm 138. When I came to verse 8, it seemed as if God Himself spoke to me through the inspired words of the psalmist: 'The Lord will fulfill his purpose for me. . . .'

"After reading that and pondering on it for a few minutes, I wrote in the margin of my Bible: 'There is tremendous comfort in knowing that my life and future are in God's hands. It frees me from the politics of ambition. If God promises to fulfill His purposes for me, I do not have to strive to advance myself. *Obedient faithfulness is all that is required of me.'*"

As a sincere believer, you are probably wondering how you can ever be sure about your motives. There is undoubtedly a heaviness in your stomach, an uneasiness that wasn't there a few minutes ago. Take hope! The very fact that you are asking those kinds of painful questions speaks well of you. Ambitious, self-serving believers are seldom, if ever, bothered with such concerns. They simply brush them aside and plunge ahead.

I don't suppose any of us can be absolutely certain that we serve God truly for God's sake. Still, there are some questions we can ask ourselves which will help us examine our motives. Probably none is more pointed than the one which asks: "Would I continue to do what I am doing if nobody saw and nobody knew? That is, would I do this if there were nothing in it for me?"

Alexander Whyte says, ". . .there is not one public man in a thousand, politician or preacher, who will go on living and working and praying out of sight, and all the time with sweetness, and contentment, and good-will, and a quiet heart."[1]

He then tells of a despairing missionary to the drunken navvies [laborers] on a new railway who complained to him. It seems a well-known preacher was vacationing in the area and would not give a single hour to minister in the tiny mission. Whyte concludes, "there is an element. . .of Simon

Magus, the Samaritan mountebank, in all public men . . . in every minister."[2]

Things may not be quite as grim as he perceives, but I fear he is closer to the truth than most of us would care to admit. Whyte's advice, although given a century ago, is still relevant today. He says: ". . . seek obscurity, for your soul's salvation lies there. If you are a popular preacher, flee from crowded churches, and hold services in bothies [cottages], and in poorhouses, and in barns, and in kitchens. . . . Starve the self-seeking quack that is still within you."[3]

Perhaps the best example, I've ever encountered, of this kind of selfless ministry was related by Walter Wangerin, Jr., the pastor of a small inner-city congregation in Evansville, Indiana. He writes autobiographically:

"Arthur lived in a shotgun house, ... More properly, Arthur lived in the front room of his house. Or rather, to speak the cold, disturbing truth, Arthur lived in a rotting stuffed chair in that room, from which he seldom stirred the last year of his life. . . .

"After several months of chair-sitting, both Arthur and his room were filthy. I do not exaggerate: roaches flowed from my step like puddles stomped in; they dropped casually from the walls. I stood very still. The TV flickered constantly. There were newspapers strewn all over the floor. There lay a damp film on every solid object in the room, from which arose a close, moldly odor, as though it were alive and sweating. But the dampness was a blessing, because Arthur smoked.

"He had a bottom lip like a shelf. Upon that shelf he placed lit cigarettes, and then he did not remove them again until they had burned quite down, at which moment he blew them toward a television set. Burning, they hit the newspapers on the floor. But it is impossible to ignite a fine, moist mildew. Blessedly, they went out.

"Then the old man would sharpen the sacrifice of my visit. Motioning toward a foul and oily sofa, winking as though he knew what mortal damage such a compost could do to my linens and my dignity, he said in hostly tones: 'Have a seat, why don't you, Reverend?'

"From the beginning I did not like to visit Arthur Forte.

"Nor did he make my job (my ministry! you cry. My service! My discipleship! No — just my job) any easier. He did not wish a quick psalm, a professional prayer, devotions. Rather, he wanted acutely to dispute a young clergyman's faith. Seventy years a churchgoer, the old man narrowed his eye at me and debated the goodness of God. . . . And I was a fumbling, lubberly sort to be defending the Almighty —

"When I left him, I was empty in my soul and close to tears, and testy, my own faith seeming most stale, flat, unprofitable at the moment. *I didn't like to visit Arthur.*

"The man was, by late summer, failing. He did not remove himself from the chair to let me in (I entered an unlocked door), nor even to pass urine (which entered a chair impossibly seamy). The August heat was unbearable and dangerous to one in his condition; therefore, I argued that Arthur go to the hospital despite his criticisms of the place.

"But he had a better idea, ho, ho! He took off all his clothes.

"Naked, Arthur greeted me. Naked, finally, the old man asked my prayers and the devout performance of private worship — and we prayed. Naked, too, he demanded Communion. Oh, these were not the conditions I had imagined. It is an embarrassing thing, to put bread into the mouth of a naked man: 'My body, my blood,' and Arthur's belly and his groin — He'd raised the level of my sacrifice to anguish. I was mortified.

"And still he was not finished.

"For in those latter days, the naked Arthur Forte asked me, his pastor, to come forward and put his slippers on, his undershorts and his pants. And I did. His feet had begun to swell, so it caused him (and me!) terrible pain in those personal moments when I took his hard heel in my hands and worked a splitbacked slipper round it. He groaned out loud when he stood to take the clothing one leg at a time. And he leaned on me, and I put my arm around his naked back and I drew the pants up his naked leg and I groaned and deep, deep in my soul I groaned. We hurt, he and I. But his was the sacrifice beyond my telling it. In those moments I came to know a certain wordless affection for Arthur Forte.

"Now read me your words, 'ministry,' and 'service,' and 'discipleship,' for then I began to understand them: then, at the touching of Arthur's feet, when that and nothing else was all that Arthur yearned for, one human being to touch him, physically to touch his old flesh, and not to judge. Holy Communion: in the most dramatic terms available, the old man had said, 'Love me.'

"...I do not suppose that Arthur consciously gave me the last year of his life, nor that he chose to teach me. Yet, by his mere being; by forcing me to take that life, real, unsweetened, barenaked, hurting and critical; by demanding that I serve him altogether unrewarded; by wringing from me first mere gestures of loving and then the love itself — but a sacrificial love, a Christ-like love, being love for one so indisputably unlovable — he did prepare me for my ministry....

"And the first flush of that experience is, generally, a sense of failure; *for this sort of ministry severely diminishes the minister, makes him insignificant, makes him the merest servant, the least in the transaction.* To feel so small is to feel somehow failing, weak, unable.

"But there, right there, begins true servanthood: The disciple who has, despite himself, denied himself....

"In the terrible, terrible doing of ministry is the minister born. And, curiously, the best teachers of that nascent minister are sometimes the neediest people, foul to touch, unworthy, ungiving, unlovely, yet haughty in demanding — and then miraculously receiving — love. These poor, forever with us, are our riches."[4] (emphasis mine)

A person cannot minister (serve) under those conditions unless he is willing to constantly die to self. In the first place, he ministers unseen, out of the public eye. There is nothing in it to gratify his flesh. This type of ministry is gruesome rather than glamorous. It humiliates the minister long before it exalts him. And even his exalting is not the outward display of the flesh, but the inner exalting of the spiritual man. You can be sure that Simon Magnus would not offer money for this gift.

This ministry, like all true ministry, grows out of relationship with God. Our motives, if not altogether pure, are at least being purified by our relationship with the Lord and by the ministry itself. By being much with God, we become much like God, and now our hearts beat in holy harmony with His. What touches Him touches us. His concerns become our concerns. Now we work for the coming of His Kingdom, rather than for the advancement of our own.

Several years ago my missionary brother and his family were returning home from the mission field for a brief furlough. As they were leaving their adopted country, Don's wife, Melba, began to weep.

Gently he asked, "What's wrong, Sweetheart?"

Through her tears she managed to say, "It feels like we're going the wrong way."

So completely had she committed her heart to the doing of God's work, without regard for personal recognition or reward, that even a well-deserved rest rent her heart. On the mission field there were few of the conveniences of life in the United States. There they were involved in the difficult work of church planting, for which efforts they received little, if any, recognition. In America they would be welcomed by family and friends. They would be honored for their sacrificial labor. Still, all she longed for was the opportunity to continue their anonymous ministry. Her deepest joy came, not in recognition or the acclaim of men, but in doing the will of the Father.

I share Melba's experience because I think it illustrates the holy thing that happens when one works *with* God rather than just *for* God. Often when we work for God, our work (ministry) becomes secondary to our "success" and the personal recognition it brings. When we work with God, the work itself becomes a means of grace, an instrument of His righteousness, shaping us to His likeness. Or as Thomas Kelly writes in *A Testament of Devotion*, "there is a sense in which, in this terrible tenderness, we become one with God and bear in our quivering souls the sins and burdens, the benightedness and the tragedy of the creatures of the whole world, and suffer in their suffering, and die in their death."[5]

When this happens, we are finally nearing that place where we truly "love God for God's sake." Simon Magnus is dead, or at least, dying, and in his place a true servant is being born.

Endnotes

[1]Alexander Whyte, D.D., *Bible Characters* (Grand Rapids: Zondervan Publishing House, 1967), p. 122.

[2]Ibid.

[3]Ibid., p. 124.

[4]Walter Wangerin, Jr., *Ragman and Other Cries of Faith* (San Francisco: Harper & Row Publishers, Inc., 1984), pp. 65-71.

[5]Thomas R. Kelly, *A Testament of Devotion,* quoted in *Disciplines for the Inner Life* by Bob Benson and Michael W. Benson (Waco: Word Books, 1985), p. 279.

Chapter 5

REDEEMING YOUR DIFFICULTIES

Some years ago I heard a gifted Bible teacher say, "God allows some things to happen *to us* in order to do something *in us* so He can do something *through us.*" Nowhere is this truth more clearly illustrated than in the life of Jacob's favorite son, Joseph.

His destiny was never in doubt. He was clearly ordained to be a ruler, but a considerable amount of water would pass under the bridge before this gifted young man would become the second most powerful man in all of Egypt. Not infrequently God uses a combination of spiritual experiences and painful adversity to mold us into the kind of men and women He can use in the Kingdom. " 'Oh,' cried Samuel Rutherford, 'what I owe to the file, and the hammer, and the furnace of my Lord Jesus!' "[1]

In Joseph's life, as is often the case, the adversity was more of his own making than God's. When he was just seventeen, God gave him two prophetic dreams. In the first he was in the field with his brothers, binding up sheaves of grain. Suddenly his sheaf stood upright and his brothers' sheaves gathered around it and bowed down to it. His second dream was not unlike the first. This time the sun and moon and eleven stars were bowing down to him.

Now that would be heady stuff for anyone, and Joseph was no exception. The humility and good judgment which would characterize his later administration as the prime minister of Egypt was sadly lacking at this point in his life. As a consequence, his youthful pride set in motion a series of events which appeared tragic at the time, but later proved to be the very thing that God used to make him into the godly man we now so highly esteem.

First, his brothers, inflamed to jealousy by both their father's favoritism and Joseph's unabashed recounting of his dreams, sold him to a group of Ishmaelite slave traders. They, in turn, sold him to Potiphar, the captain of Pharaoh's guards. According to the Scriptures, Joseph was ". . .well-built and handsome" (Gen. 39:6), and this proved to be his undoing. Potiphar's wife was attracted to him and propositioned him, not once but several times. When it finally became apparent that he was not going to succumb to her charms, she became vindictive. She told her husband that Joseph had attempted to rape her and that she had escaped only by screaming for help.

"When. . .(he) heard the story his wife told him. . .he burned with anger. Joseph's master took him and put him in prison, the place where the king's prisoners were confined" (Gen. 39:19,20).

Joseph had now suffered two unspeakable tragedies, either of which would be enough to destroy a lesser man. Yet as gifted as he was, it was not his personal resiliency which enabled him to overcome, but the faithfulness of his father's God! The Scriptures tell us that when he was taken into Potiphar's household as a slave, *"The LORD was with Joseph* and he prospered. . ."* (Gen. 39:2). We also read that later, ". . .while Joseph was there in the prison, *the LORD was with him;* he showed him kindness and granted him favor in the eyes of the prison warden" (Gen. 39:20,21). Joseph was able to overcome these seemingly insurmountable setbacks because he knew the Lord was with him.

We, too, can endure any hardship, overcome any difficulty, as long as we can be assured that God is with us. What we cannot endure is the thought of facing life's vicissitudes alone. Yet it is at this very point that many of us lose heart. Somewhere we have picked up the notion that if we live a faithful and obedient life, we will be spared the pain and sorrow that is so much a part of our fallen world. Such an idea is neither Christian nor scriptural and sets us up for some devastating disappointments. When we equate all suffering with the absence of God, or at least with His disapproval, we leave ourselves open to unspeakable temptations. At the very time we need most to be assured of God's love and faithfulness, our theology leaves us with nothing but tormenting questions.

Undoubtedly, our attitude toward suffering is a decisive factor in how it will affect us. In *For God's Sake, Be Human,* John Killinger relates a story told by the philosopher Tagore which illustrates this point. He tells about a game which a little girl played with him:

"She asked him to imagine that he was shut up in a room that had been locked from the outside and to tell her how he was going to get out. He said that he would call for help. But she was not willing for him to get out so easily; she promptly replied that all help had been removed from the area. He said then that he would kick the door down. She promptly made the door into a steel one. Each time he proposed some solution to his dilemma, she invented some additional impediment to his escape."[2]

Killinger then concludes: "Thus it is in life. There are times when we are blocked at every turn. Whatever solution we devise to our problems, we come immediately upon some new difficulty. How a man accepts difficulty, then, becomes all important. If a man is cowardly and complains all the time about his lot in life, he has chosen one way of living. But he need not choose this way. He can regard conflict as a natural part of existence and meet it with resolution and ingenuity."[3]

Better yet, he can regard it as an instrument of grace to "make him" all that God intends him to be. Not that God wills his suffering, but that he uses it (that is, He redeems it and causes it to contribute to his ultimate Christlikeness). Joseph affirms this truth when he tells his brothers, "You intended to harm me, but God intended it for good to accomplish what is now being done, the saving of many lives" (Gen. 50:20).

In Romans, Chapter 8, Paul expounds this same principle: "And we know that *in all things God works* for the good of those who love him, who have been called according to his purpose" (Rom. 8:28). (emphasis mine) Once again the focus is, not upon the circumstances in which a person finds himself, but upon the faithfulness of the God Who works in all things for the good of those who love Him.

A common mistake, in times of difficulty and disappointment, is to try to figure out how God is working (that is, what good He is bringing out of all our suffering). It is a mistake, because, for the most part, His ways are far beyond anything we might imagine. In fact, trying to discover His ultimate purpose in such situations often leads either to absurd conclusions or to outright despair. For example, the way God worked in Joseph's life was obvious only in retrospect. Who could have imagined how He would weave slavery, false accusations and imprisonment into His grand design? It certainly wasn't the most likely course to political power, even in ancient Egypt.

Therefore, when you find yourself in the midst of some unspeakable adversity, don't try to figure out how God is going to use it, just trust Him. Often His wisdom is past finding out (that is, it is beyond our finite understanding). I remember a touching incident some years ago which drove this truth home to me.

A young couple in our church was expecting their first baby, and they wanted everything to be perfect. All through the pregnancy they prayed for their unborn child — for perfect health, for a gentle disposition and for a spiritual aptitude. When the baby was born, it seemed that their prayers had been ignored. She was a cranky child and cried almost incessantly. When she was just a few weeks old, the doctor discovered a hernia and scheduled her for surgery.

Needless to say, all of this was almost more than the young parents could bear. In real frustration they came to see me. Why, they demanded, had God not answered their prayers? They had prayed in faith. They had done everything they knew to do, so why hadn't it "worked"? Of course, I had no answers, at least none that were acceptable to them, and as a result their visit only deepened their depression.

The day of the surgery arrived, and I met the couple at the hospital. Long before I located the parents I could hear the baby wailing. Her anguished cries echoed forlornly down the long hospital corridors. Turning a final corner, I saw the young mother nervously pacing the hallway, trying to comfort her baby. Almost immediately I realized what was happening. The baby was hungry. Following the doctor's orders, the parents had not given her anything to eat since ten o'clock the night before. By now she had missed at least two feedings, and she refused to be assuaged.

With a flash of insight, which I believe came from the Holy Spirit, I realized this was the answer to their "why" questions. I walked up to the mother and asked her what was wrong with the baby. She explained that the child was hungry.

"Why don't you feed her?" I asked.

Giving me a look that obviously questioned my intelligence, she impatiently replied that the baby couldn't have anything to eat before surgery.

"Well, at least explain that to her," I answered. "She obviously thinks you're a sadist. I mean, you carry her in your arms next to your breast. It must be obvious to her that you could feed her if you wanted to, if you cared."

By now the mother was sure that I had lost my mind, but she decided to humor me. In a condescending tone, she patiently explained that the baby was far too young to understand such logical reasoning. In fact, the baby didn't even understand spoken words yet.

Gently, I said, "I know that what you are doing is out of love. I know you have your baby's best interest at heart, and so do you. But your baby doesn't understand that, and there's no way you can explain it to her."

Understanding began to brighten her tense features, so I continued: "That's the way it is with God. He is too wise to ever make a mistake, and too loving to ever cause one of His children needless pain. Still, He must sometimes risk our misunderstanding in order to do what's best for us. We are simply too young, too finite, too human, to comprehend His infinite wisdom. I can't always tell you why God does what He does, but I can assure you that He is trustworthy!"

Am I saying that God afflicted that couple's infant daughter in order to develop character in their lives? No! Not on your life. Did God allow it? Perhaps. For certain He is working in it. And He will redeem it (that is, cause it to contribute to the development of their spiritual character). That's the hope I have. That's where my faith is fixed — in the eternal craftsmanship of God. In His remarkable ability to take the senseless tragedies of life and touch them with His grace, redeem them, and ultimately use them. I trust the love and faithfulness of God which is at work in all things. I don't necessarily understand it, but I trust Him.

Endnotes

[1]James S. Stewart, *The Wind of the Spirit* (Nashville: Abingdon Press, 1968), p. 141.

[2]John Killinger, *For God's Sake, Be Human* (Waco: Word Books, 1970), p. 138.

[3]Ibid.

Chapter 6

THE DIVINE TASK
"The Making of the Man of God"

"When I was very young," writes Chaim Potok in *The Chosen,* "my father, may he rest in peace, began to wake me in the middle of the night just so I would cry. I was a child, but he would wake me and tell me stories about the destruction of Jerusalem and the sufferings of the people of Israel, and I would cry. For years he did this. Once he took me to visit the poor, the beggars, to listen to them talk. My father himself never talked to me, except when we studied together. *He taught me with silence.* He taught me to look into myself, to find my own strength, to walk around inside myself in company with my soul.

"When his people would ask him why he was so silent with his son, he would say to them that he did not like to talk, words are cruel, words play tricks, they distort what is in the heart, they conceal the heart, the heart speaks through silence. One learns of the pain of others by suffering one's own pain, he would say, by turning inside oneself, by finding one's own soul. And it is important to know of pain, he said. It destroys our self-pride, our arrogance, our indifference toward others. It makes us aware of how frail and tiny we are and of how much we must depend upon the Master of the Universe. Only slowly, very slowly, did I begin to understand what he was saying. *For years his silence bewildered and frightened me, though I always trusted him, I never hated him.*"[1]

What a thought! How often I have said to the Lord: "God Almighty, why don't You speak to me? God Almighty, Your silence frightens me!" But I tell you the absolute truth, and I do not exaggerate. No matter how deep the night, no matter how awful the silence, I always trusted Him. And slowly, ever so slowly, over months and sometimes years, I came to understand the wisdom of His silence. Some of the mysteries of God, some of the holiness of life, are simply too sacred for words. The most profound and holy things God has ever communicated to me were simply communicated as deep calling to deep. And even at this moment, as I write this, there are no words for the things I have learned. There are no road maps to the places I've gone. Oh, the wisdom of Almighty God!

"And when I was old enough to understand," Potok continues, "he told me that of all people a tzaddik (a righteous, wise man) especially must know of pain. A tzaddik must know how to suffer for his people, he said. He must take their pain from them and carry it on his own shoulder. He must cry, in his heart he must always cry. Even when he dances and sings, he must cry for the sufferings of his people."[2]

And that's how it is for those of us who would know God and who would minister for Him. Even as we dance and sing, celebrating the holy love of God, there is another part of us that cries for the suffering and grieving in the Body of Christ. There's another part of us that wanders the empty hallways of hospitals the world over weeping with those who suffer so cruelly. Even as we sing the great hymns of the Church, celebrating God's eternal faithfulness, there is another part of us that is bowed down with the grief of all humanity. And it is this brokenness, this spiritual sorrow, which is our rite of passage into the ministry. He who enters by any other door is not a true minister, but an insincere poseur.

"'I will not listen to any man,' said Richard Baxter after he had gone through a great sorrow, 'who has not felt what I have felt.'"[3]

Surely this is what James S. Stewart, the Scottish preacher, meant when he said, "In Love's service only the wounded soldiers can serve."[4]

William Barclay, the gifted English scholar, testifies to this truth as well. He writes: "My mother died of cancer of the spine in such a way and out of such a pain that it was a relief to see her release. She was a saint, and the sorrow was very sore. But I can remember my father coming to me to this day and saying to me: 'You will have a new note in your preaching now.' And it was so, in the goodness of God, because I was better able to help others who were going through it, because I had gone through it."[5]

What am I saying? Simply that nothing happens to us in this life that God cannot redeem. That's the miracle of grace, the miracle of God's love! There is nothing, absolutely nothing, the enemy can do to us, nothing life can do to us, that God cannot redeem. And I believe with all my heart that we can somehow endure anything if we know that it won't be wasted. We can endure anything for Jesus' sake if we can just be assured that God will redeem it and use it for His glory.

Helen Roseveare, who served for many years in the Belgian Congo as a missionary doctor with the Worldwide Evangelism Crusade, shared a touching incident which drives this truth home. She said: "A young missionary couple during their first term of service in a foreign land were expecting their first baby. The mother wrote to me from the hospital a few days after the birth to tell me that her baby had died....She went on in her letter, 'Local women whom I've been trying to reach with the gospel visited me yesterday, and their loving sympathy was very touching. Then one of them said to me, "Now you are the same as us. Now we will listen to what you tell us." I find my heart rising above my sorrow....I can identify with the local community in their daily sufferings and so be able to share Christ with them.'"[6]

The Apostle Paul affirms this same truth: "Now I want you to know, brothers, that what has happened to me has really served to advance the gospel" (Phil. 1:12). When Paul penned those words, he was a prisoner in Rome facing possible execution. Yet, rather than succumbing to despair, he affirmed his faith in the eternal craftsmanship of the God he served!

He then lists several ways his imprisonment has served to advance the Gospel. First, it has become obvious to everyone connected with the palace guard that Paul is in chains, not because he is a criminal, but because he is a Christian. Second, as a result of his witness, several members of Caesar's household have been converted. (See Phil. 4:22.)

Not only has his witness from prison resulted in the conversion of members of the palace guard and Caesar's household, it has also encouraged other believers ". . .to speak the word of God more courageously and fearlessly" (Phil. 1:14). Paul then adds: ". . .The important thing is that in every way,. . .Christ is preached. And because of this I rejoice" (Phil. 1:18).

As significant as these advances were, they are almost inconsequential compared to the most significant contribution Paul's imprisonment afforded the Church. I am referring, of course, to his prison epistles. Without this "forced idleness," Paul might have stayed so busy planting new churches that he could not have found time to write his letters, which make up a substantial portion of the body of material we now call the New Testament!

All of this seems so obvious in retrospect, as does the way God used the adversity in Joseph's life, but at the time it was not evident at all. Put yourself in the place of these two men. It wouldn't be hard to despair given their circumstances. I mean, it must have seemed that God had forsaken them.

Often we read the Scriptures so casually, so superficially, that we miss everything that's not spelled out in black and white. For instance, nothing was ever said about the emotional trauma which Joseph surely experienced as the result of his brothers' betrayal and his imprisonment. And because it isn't mentioned, we tend to assume he was immune to such emotions (that is, if we consider it at all).

But was he immune? Did he sail merrily through life, like some kind of simpleton, oblivious to its cruel injustices? I think not. Read Alex Haley's *Roots* and see how it feels to be sold into slavery. Read *A Time To Die* by Tom Wicker and sense the anger and hatred which seethes behind prison walls. If the prophet Elijah was ". . . a man subject to like passions as we are. . ." (James 5:17 KJV), wasn't Joseph too? If Jesus was "in all points tempted like as we are. . ." (Heb. 4:15 KJV), isn't it logical to think that Joseph had to deal with his own ugly emotions? And doesn't his eventual triumph become more meaningful in light of the struggle?

The next question then is: How did Joseph handle his feelings? Once again, Genesis is silent. We have no specific scriptural record of what Joseph did to overcome his anger and hatred, but we do have some scriptural principles which show us how to overcome our own unholy emotions.

The key word is forgive. To *forgive* means "to let go" — to let go of the hurts, the grudges, the feelings, even the memories associated with an unhappy past event. As long as we are constantly reliving the hurtful incidents of our past, either in memory or in conversation, we haven't fully released them or truly forgiven the persons who caused them.

We know that Joseph let go of his anger and hatred — we know he forgave his brothers, Potiphar, even

Potiphar's wife — because he never talks about the past, never spends precious time or energy plotting revenge or dreaming about what might have been. Only once, in all of Genesis, does he refer to what has happened to him, and then only as a necessary explanation.

Joseph's whole adult life is a living testimony to the redemptive touch of God manifested through a surrendered life. He let go of his anger and bitterness; consequently, he was free to get on with the business of living as God's person in the world. When his God-given dreams were finally fulfilled, when his brothers knelt before him, when he held their lives in his hand, he was not even tempted to harm them.

"But Joseph said to them, 'Don't be afraid. Am I in the place of God? You intended to harm me, but God intended it for good to accomplish what is now being done, the saving of many lives. So then, don't be afraid. I will provide for you and your children.' And he reassured them and spoke kindly to them" (Gen. 50:19-21).

Because Joseph trusted God with his unspeakable sufferings (that is, because he surrendered them to the Lord and remained faithful under even the most adverse circumstances), God was able to do something in him and eventually through him. As Joseph Parker wrote many years ago, " 'Adversity makes or mars a man.' "[7] In Joseph's case, it was used by God to make him.

During the Simba uprising of the sixties, Helen Roseveare was savagely beaten and gang-raped by the guerrillas. She was able to survive that terrible night because she believed that God would redeem her sufferings (that is, use them for eternal good).

"Ten years later," she writes, "while I spoke to a university Christian group, God prompted me to allude to the suffering of rape, the most dreaded experience of any girl or woman....At the close, when all but two students had left the hall, one of them came to me and asked if I would speak to her teen-age sister. 'She was raped five weeks ago,' the older girl explained, 'and none of us can reach through to help her. For five weeks she has not spoken to anyone.' I turned and looked at the younger girl, who slowly started toward me.

"She quickened her pace, ran to me, threw her arms around my neck, and we cried together. Then she poured out her story in the next two hours."[8] "I looked back ten years and knew a little more of the 'why.'"[9]

As I think on these things, I believe I am coming to a new understanding of John 15:13. When Jesus says, " 'Greater love has no one than this, that one lay down his life for his friends,' " He means there will be times in our lives when we will deliberately give up our "right" to a miracle for the greater good of the Kingdom. Times when we will choose suffering and sorrow rather than a personal deliverance so that the greater good of the Kingdom might be advanced!

In Helen Roseveare's case, she chose to trust God with her unspeakable tragedy rather than blame Him for the things she had suffered. It was ten long years before she had even a hint of how God might use it for eternal good. Still she trusted Him. In the light of that teen-ager's response some of the good is now obvious. By living through that tragic experience and finding the sufficiency of God's grace to continue her life and ministry, she was in a unique position to help that terrified teen-aged girl who had also been raped. A testimony of divine deliverance could not have reached that victim. It would have only reinforced her bitterness and distrust. Helen's experience, on the other hand, encouraged her to believe that God could redeem her devastating ordeal as well.

If a person is still loving God for self's sake (that is, for what he can get out of it), then adversity, especially of that magnitude, will likely destroy his faith, or at least embitter him. But for those, like Helen Roseveare, who have matured beyond that stage, tribulation and misfortune often provide an opportunity for God to transform their character (that is, "make them" into the kind of persons who are uniquely fit for the Master's service).

Rollo May writes in *The Art of Counseling*, "People then should rejoice in suffering, strange as it sounds, for this is a sign of the availability of energy to transform their characters. Suffering is nature's way of indicating a mistaken attitude or way of behavior, and....to the non-egocentric person every moment of suffering is the opportunity for growth."[10]

The writer of the epistle to the Hebrews counsels us: "Endure hardship as discipline;....Our fathers disciplined us for a little while as they thought best; but *God disciplines us for our good, that we may share in his holiness.* No discipline seems pleasant at the time, but painful. Later on, however, it produces a harvest of righteousness and peace for those who have been trained by it" (Heb. 12:7,10,11). (emphasis mine)

We must be careful here to distinguish between discipline and punishment. Punishment is punitive, while discipline is preparatory. Punishment focuses on past mistakes and failures. Discipline, on the other hand, focuses on preparing us to correctly respond to future situations.

Let me emphasize again that God does not send adversity. It is simply a consequence of humanity's fallen state and/or our own choices. However, God does use it (that is, He transforms it, makes it discipline for our training). "Now obviously no 'chastening' seems pleasant at the time: it is in fact most unpleasant. Yet when it is all over we can see that it has quietly produced the fruit of real goodness in the characters of those who have accepted it. So tighten your loosening grip and steady your trembling knees. . ." (Heb. 12:11-13 Phillips).

Maybe the most significant change takes place in our relationship with God. In many ways it is a subtle change, and we often become aware of it only in retrospect. Heretofore, God has been a means to an end. A way of finding forgiveness, provision, even power. As a result, we never really had a relationship with Him. We "used" Him, but we did not know Him. Now God is our strength, our very life. He is the only end we seek. Consequently, we bond with Him and experience a centering of our lives. And, maybe for the very first time, we experience fulfillment in the deepest part of our person. We have come home, at last, to God.

Endnotes

[1]Chaim Potok, *The Chosen,* copyright © 1967 by Chaim Potok. Reprinted by permission of The William Morris Agency, Inc.

[2]Ibid.

[3]J. Wallace Hamilton, *Where Now Is Thy God?* (Old Tappan: Fleming H. Revell, 1969), p. 62.

[4]Stewart, p. 155.

[5]William Barclay, *The Beatitudes and The Lord's Prayer for Everyman* (New York: Harper & Row Publishers, Inc., 1968), p. 214.

[6]Helen Roseveare, "The Spirit's Enablement," quoted in *Confessing Christ as Lord: The Urbana '81 Compendium,* edited by John W. Alexander (Downer's Grove: InterVarsity Press, 1982), p. 170.

[7]Joseph Parker quoted in *Bible Paradoxes,* copyright © 1963 by R. Earl Allen, p. 39.

[8]Roseveare, p. 172.

[9]Ibid.

[10]Rollo May, *The Art of Counseling,* (New York: Abington-Cokesbury Press, 1939).

Chapter 7

THE DIVINE DESIRE
"Intimacy Not Power"

As incongruous as it may seem, the truth is, many deeply committed believers have only a "working" relationship with God. Like the older brother in the story of the prodigal, they have worked for Him all their lives, yet they do not know Him. Nor do they allow God to know them. They have mastered the tragic art of saying right things, instead of real things; of presenting their religious selves to God, rather than their real selves. As a consequence, what could have been a deeply fulfilling relationship becomes a cheap masquerade.

Please do not misunderstand me. I am not questioning the validity of their salvation or the authenticity of their ministries. For the most part, they are sincere men and women of God who have spent a lifetime "doing" things for the Lord but without ever really becoming intimate with Him. Of them Jesus might very well say, "...'Have I been with you so long, and yet you do not know me...?'" (John 14:9 RSV).

A classic example is the prophet Elijah. No one had a more powerful ministry. And he remains, even today, the most revered prophet in Israel's long history. Yet he reached a point in his life when he became suicidally depressed. The Scriptures say, "...He came to a broom tree, sat down under it and prayed that he might die. 'I have had enough, LORD,' he said. 'Take my life...'" (1 Kings 19:4).

Undoubtedly, there were a number of contributing factors, including (but not limited to) unrealistic expectations, physical and emotional exhaustion, as well as years of isolation. Still, I've concluded that the primary cause may have been his relationship with God which appears to have been built on power rather than intimacy. Considering the way God chose to minister to him while he was in the depth of his depression, I think it is a valid conclusion.

"The LORD said, 'Go out and stand on the mountain in the presence of the LORD, for the LORD is about to pass by.'

"Then a great and powerful wind tore the mountains apart and shattered the rocks before the LORD, but the LORD was not in the wind. After the wind there was an earthquake, but the LORD was not in the earthquake. After the earthquake came a fire, but the LORD was not in the fire. And after the fire came *a gentle whisper*. When Elijah heard it, he pulled his cloak over his face...."

1 Kings 19:11-13

God began the restoration process by giving Elijah a spiritual experience based on intimacy rather than power, a gentle whisper rather than a roaring wind. Why? Because power is seldom what we need when we have come to the end of ourselves. At those times, we need relationship — a gentle whisper assuring us of our value, of our place in God's Kingdom, "a still small voice" telling us of His love.

If you've ever had an experience like that, you know why Elijah covered his face. The thing you have longed for, searched for your whole life long, is finally happening. And in the most unexpected way, when you least deserve it. Jesus is there, with you, nearer than the air you breathe, more real than life itself.

Your heart cries out to Him: "Whisper to me, Jesus, because my heart is heavy. Whisper to me, Jesus, because discouragement has taken me by the throat. Whisper to me, Jesus, because I am alone and undone on the inside. Whisper to me, Jesus, because I can't bear to live another moment without You."

And then He whispers things so sweet, so holy, so tender, it seems your heart will burst. He whispers things so real, so true, so eternal, that you cannot help but cover your face. His presence is so pure you can't bear to look, and yet you must. You must, for this is the moment you've lived your whole life for. The moment when, finally, you are brought face to face with Him.

Once we have been assured of God's love, of our value to Him and of our place in His Kingdom, then He begins to address the root cause of this spiritual crisis. "...Then a voice said to him, 'What are you doing here, Elijah?'" (1 Kings 19:13).

This is the moment of truth for Elijah, and for us! The question really isn't "What are you doing here?" but more precisely "What is your name?" (that is: "Who are you? What kind of person are you? What choices have you made that brought you to this moment?")

God raises these questions, not because He doesn't know, but to bring us face to face with our real selves. In truth, God knows everything about us, nothing is hid from His eyes. Of Jeremiah He said, "'Before I formed you in the womb I knew you...'" (Jer. 1:5). Jesus declared, "'...God knows your hearts...'" (Luke 16:15).

Yet what is so obvious to God is often hidden from our eyes. It was once known to us, but over the years we have learned to edit the truth about ourselves until it is more to our liking. It isn't an outright lie so much as it is a change in perception. The "facts" remain the same, but the conclusions are totally different. We have mastered the subtle art of deception, and tragically we have become victims of our own deceit.

"Self-knowledge, the beginning of wisdom," wrote John Gardener, "is ruled out for most people by the increasingly effective self-deception they practice as they grow older. By middle age, most of us are accomplished fugitives from ourselves."[1]

Some years ago I became aware of this self-deception in my own life, and in my journal I wrote:

"Lord,
How do I go about
being honest with You,
    myself,
        others?
Deception is woven into
the very fiber of my being.*

"I rearrange circumstances and events,
like a housewife rearranging furniture,
until they are to my liking,
until I can present myself
in the best possible light.
The careful turning of a phrase,
the slightest inflection,
a perfect gesture,
and the gist of the event
is turned to my advantage
without really altering the facts.

"Once turned, I replay it
over and over again
until I begin to believe
it really happened that way,
until in my mind
it becomes the truth.

"I think
I've been honest with You,
but how can I know?
Don't let me
get away with pretending
and protesting my innocence.

---

*" 'The heart is deceitful above all things and beyond cure. Who can understand it?' "
Jeremiah 17:9

"Wrestle with me
in the dark night
of my dishonesty
until, like Jacob of old,
I come clean with You.
Face me with who I am,
what I am.
Force me
to confess and claim
my past,
    my present,
        my identity.
"Not with excuses and explanations
and other self-justifying maneuvers,
but with the courage
to trust Your love.
And with a faith which believes
such honest confession
births the intimacy
which makes me new.

"Amen."

God brings us to such moments, not to humiliate us, but to set us free. As long as we believe the deception we have created about ourselves and our lives, we are prisoners of that lie. We can have only the most superficial relationship with Him and others because the self we bring to the relationship is a false self. In truth, we are not relating to one another, but rather building an elaborate masquerade.

I understand this dilemma best when it is likened to a cast of characters in a play. On stage, the leading man and the leading lady may have a romantic relationship, they may even marry, while in real life they may have only the most superficial association. The characters they portray actually have little or nothing to do with who they really are. And their relationship in the play is not real. It is a role created by the playwrite and it has nothing to do with their real lives.

Now let's apply that analogy to our spiritual life. When we approach God with less than total honesty, we become actors playing a role. As a result, there can be no real relationship. That's bad enough in itself, but things become even more complicated when we can no longer distinguish our real self from the role we have created. The indignity is complete when we have created a characterization for God which complements our false self. Tragically, this is the case more often than I would care to believe. As a consequence, our spiritual life lacks vitality and our relationships are unfulfilling. Not infrequently we end up like Elijah, deeply depressed, without hope.

This does not mean that we are "bad" people, at least not in the sense that we usually think of bad people. In fact, we may be very good people, if our evaluation of goodness goes no deeper than surface behavior. We do not lie, at least not outrightly. Nor do we steal, or cheat on our taxes, or step out on our spouse. Yet there is something lacking, and the gnawing ache deep within cannot be denied.

Our goodness is commendable, as far as it goes, but it is hardly the quality of life our hearts hunger for. It is what Jesus called "the righteousness of the Pharisees." (Matt. 5:20.) A righteousness which is based on outward conformity rather than inward purity. We would do well to remember that Jesus said: " 'Woe to you, teachers of the law and Pharisees, you hypocrites! You clean the outside of the cup and dish, but inside they are full of greed and self-indulgence. Blind Pharisee! *First clean the inside of the cup and dish, and then the outside also will be clean'"* (Matt. 23:25,26). (emphasis mine)

Jesus is saying that true righteousness manifests itself from the inside out. It is more than a simple behaviorial change; it is the transformation of the inner man. Yet such a transformation cannot occur until we are honest with ourselves and transparent before the Lord.

Endnotes

[1]John Gardener, *"Self-Renewal,"* quoted in *Rebuilding Your Broken World* by Gordon MacDonald (Nashville: Oliver Nelson, A Division of Thomas Nelson Publishers, 1988), p. 74.

Chapter 8

THE DIVINE GOAL
"A Transparent Relationship"

To be honest with ourselves means to see ourselves as God sees us. No more duplicity or self-deception. Now we search our hearts before the Lord and "name" ourselves (that is: we admit, to ourselves, that we are not always what we pretend to be). Once we have done this, we can be transparent before the Lord. We can now confess to Him what we have finally admitted to ourselves.

Initially, the thought of such honesty, the thought of such soul-searching, is more than a little disquieting. Most of us would prefer to "let sleeping dogs lie." Yet such an option is no option at all for the person who yearns to know God and to be known by Him. Such a person looks his fear in the eye and prays:

"Search me, O God, and know my heart (the real
me);
     test me and know my anxious thoughts.
See if there is any offensive way in me,
     and lead me in the way everlasting."
                              Psalm 139:23,24

The inward journey will be new for many of us, and
being new it will be unfamiliar, and being unfamiliar it will
likely be frightening. Even those of us who have come this
way before find it a little disconcerting at times. The things
we discover about ourselves can be painful beyond words.
Yet we continue, for as unsettling as the process is, it is the
only hope we have of truly becoming men and women of
God.

Teilhard de Chardin wrote of his inward journey in
the most solemn terms: "For the first time in my life perhaps
(although I am supposed to meditate every day!), I took
the lamps and leaving the zone of everyday occupations and
relationships where everything seems clear, I went down
into my inmost self, to the deep abyss whence I feel dimly
that my power of action emanates. But as I moved further
and further away from the conventional certainties by which
social life is superficially illuminated, I became aware that
I was losing contact with myself. At each step of the descent
a new person was disclosed within me of whose name I was
no longer sure. And who no longer obeyed me. And when
I had to stop my exploration because the path faded from
beneath my steps, I found a bottomless abyss at my feet,
and out of it came — arising I know not from where —
the current which I dare to call my life."[1]

Such fearless self-honesty is not possible apart from
the presence of God. The journey is simply too great for

us. To see ourselves as we truly are would be devastating were it not for the grace of God which shows us what we are destined to be in Him. Even as we cringe at the revelation of our unabashed carnality, our shameless self-interest, He gives us a glimpse of what we can be in Christ Jesus. And this vision of our transformed self, coupled with the holy presence of the Lord, gives us the faith and the courage to stand before Him transparent.

If a person's spiritual identity and security (his righteousness) is based on his personal performance, then it will be almost impossible for him to honestly acknowledge his true thoughts and feelings. To his way of thinking, to do so, when many of them are so blatantly sinful, would be to risk losing his salvation. Consequently, he ends up lying to himself and to God. A more acceptable way of putting it might be to say that he ends up denying his true feelings.

Such denial provides a momentary reprieve, but it is just an illusion. Underneath he is still tormented with thoughts of unworthiness, and tries all the harder to deny his obvious shortcomings. If he continues this pattern of behavior long enough, he becomes self-deceived. His un-Christlike characteristics cease to concern him. In fact, he no longer searches his heart or examines his motives, at least not in more than a cursory way.

Yet this self-deception is not without its price. It takes tremendous energy to keep our feelings repressed. If we relax our constant vigilance for even a moment, a host of tormenting thoughts and self-doubts assail us. Even when we manage to maintain our facade, these repressed emotions have a way of popping up at the most inopportune times. Usually they are disguised as legitimate concerns, but upon closer examination their true source becomes apparent. And such misplaced emotions have a tendency to wreak havoc with our relationships.

Even if we manage to escape the aforementioned pitfalls, we cannot hope to experience the fulfillment for which our hearts hunger. The desperate need to be right, to always appear in the best possible light, keeps us from building intimate relationships. We dare not risk letting anyone know us, for they might discover that we are not the persons we appear to be. Even in our closest relationships, with God and family, we are reserved, we keep people at arm's distance. Such reserve may be safe, but it is not fulfilling.

How, then, does a person go about becoming honest with himself and with God? How do we overcome our fears and the duplicity of a lifetime? There are no easy answers, no shortcuts. But for the sincere believer, the path is increasingly clear.

Before we can allow God to know us, we must know Him. And in knowing Him we come to understand the nature of our salvation and the source of our security. Our righteousness is not based on our personal performance, but on the finished work of Jesus Christ. His sinless life has been imparted to us; therefore, His righteousness has become our righteousness. Once we understand this truth, we no longer have to deny our inconsistencies or pretend that we are something we are not.

Second Corinthians 5:21 declares, "God made him (Jesus) who had no sin to be sin for us, so that in him we might become the righteousness of God."

How was Jesus made to "be sin for us"? By committing sin? Hardly! He was ". . .tempted in every way, just as we are — yet was without sin" (Heb. 4:15).

The Sinless One was made to be sin for us by *an act of God.* God took the sinfulness of fallen humanity and imparted it to Jesus. With that sovereign act, our sinfulness became His sinfulness, our "sin" (that is: who we were, our fallen nature) became Who He was — "God made him who had no sin *to be sin. . .*" (2 Cor. 5:21). (emphasis mine)

How then do we become "the righteousness of God" in Him? By living sinless lives? By walking in personal righteousness? Of course not! Jesus was not made sin by sinning, and we are not made righteous by our good works. *It is an act of God!* When we express faith in the saving work of Jesus Christ, God imparts to us the righteousness of Christ. And we who were not righteous are made the righteousness of God in Him. "All this is God's doing. . ." (2 Cor. 5:18 Phillips).

It is impossible to fully define the mysteries of grace, but in order to come to a working knowledge of our salvation, we must make an attempt. Therefore, let me distinguish between what I call our *positional standing in Christ* and our *experiential life in Christ.*

Positionally, we are complete in Christ at the moment of conversion. (Col. 2:10.) Our righteousness is perfect because it is the righteousness of God. (2 Cor. 5:21.) As long as we remain in relationship with Christ Jesus, our positional standing does not change. It does not improve, no matter how godly we live, for it is already perfect. Nor is it threatened when we fail, as we are all prone to do, for it is not based on our personal performance. It is dependent on nothing but our faith in the finished work of Christ (that is, what He has done for us)!

Experientially, however, we are babies in Christ. (1 Pet. 2:2.) Paul writes, "Brothers, I could not address you as spiritual but as worldly — *mere infants* in Christ" (1 Cor. 3:1). And as immature believers we continue to react with carnal attitudes and self-centered desires. We fall prey to temptation and become ensnared in the things of the world.

On the experiential level then, while we are a new creation in Christ (2 Cor. 5:17), there is not necessarily a corresponding Christlikeness in our daily lives or in our relationships. Experientially, we are in the process of *becoming* what we already *are* positionally. This is Christ's continuing work *in* us. And, like Paul, we are ". . .confident of this, that he who began a good work in. . .(us) will carry it on to completion. . ." (Phil. 1:6).

The difficulties arise when a believer looks to his experiential life in Christ for his security, rather than to his positional standing in Him. In short, he trusts in his daily life, his own righteousness, as the basis for his relationship with God. Since no one can measure up to the standards required to merit such a relationship, either he will fall into condemnation and eventually despair, or he will deny his sinfulness and become self-righteous and self-deceived.

However, when a person sees God as a merciful heavenly Father, Who has made perfect provision for his salvation, he is free to come before Him, totally transparent and completely honest. Since his right standing with God is based on the finished work of Christ, and not his own performance, he need not fear being rejected. And freed from the fear of rejection, he can honestly acknowledge his deep need, and receive the grace of God that both redeems and renews.

Thus, when Elijah finally stands in the presence of God, he is able, at last, to articulate his heretofore undefined feelings. Until now he has been unwilling to acknowledge them, let alone examine them. Although he has never allowed them to take shape, he is quite positive that they are not the kinds of feelings a prophet should have. But now, standing in the presence of God, hearing the gentle whisper of His love, he feels the release to explore his inner struggle.

Like Teilhard de Chardin, he takes the "lamp of the LORD" (Prov. 20:27), and, leaving the zone of everyday occupations and relationships, he goes down into his inmost self, to the deep abyss from whence the true motives of his life emanate.

For years I too have endeavored to make this inward journey, and I believe I have been successful on occasion. My confidence is not in myself, but in the Lord Who goes before me. We are not talking about morbid introspection, but the deep and revealing work of the Holy Spirit which makes all things new. The Bible declares:

> "The lamp of the LORD searches the spirit of a man; it searches out his inmost being."
>
> Proverbs 20:27

My methods may be different from yours, but in order to deal specifically with the things the Holy Spirit is revealing to me, I must record them in my journal. This does two things. First, it forces me to discipline myself, to specifically name and define the issues the Spirit has identified. For instance, I recently found myself wrestling with some inconsistencies in my spiritual life and in my relationships. Of that experience I wrote:

"Lord,
Enable me to see myself as You see me.
Reveal the selfishness I cannot see,
the materialism I've overlooked,
the pride I'm unaware of.
Reveal these to me,
painful and shaming though they be.
"I stand naked before You,
here in the light of Your terrible love.
I see things I don't want to see.
Areas of weakness and failure —

"The need to share my interpersonal conflicts
in order to rally support for my position,
even if it casts others in a poor light.

"A crippling need to be liked and admired,
which makes it nearly impossible for me
to exercise firm leadership.

"A measure of professional jealousy.

Ego — 'I' problems.

"O Lord,
my faults and shortcomings are so many.
They threaten to overwhelm me.
Give me some measure of hope,
just a glimpse of what I can be
when Your grace has done its holy work.

"Amen."

Alone, we are no match for these subterranean forces. With Jeremiah we must all acknowledge:

> " 'The heart is deceitful above all things
> and beyond cure. Who can understand it?' "
>
> Jeremiah 17:9

Yet with God's help we can take captive these inner enemies. As the wise man wrote:

> "The crucible for silver and the furnace
>   for gold,
> but the LORD tests (reveals and purifies) the heart."
>
> Proverbs 17:3

The second thing the journal does is give me a bench mark, a record of God's dealings in my life. "The process is like watching the growth of a child. If one is with them each day it will be hard to see them growing. It is only as we measure them against a mark on the doorpost or try to fit them into last spring's clothes that we realize the extent of their growth. And even though the process may be imperceptible to us at a given moment we will begin to note by reading back through our journal or by sensing our responses and attitudes in everyday matters and relationships that he is changing us and endowing us with the fruits of his spirit."[2]

Although the inward journey is obviously difficult, it is the only way to fully experience the spiritual life and fellowship that is promised in Christ. God can only deliver us from the things we confess, and we can only confess those things that we have allowed the Spirit to make known to us. As long as we deny their existence, or refuse to identify them specifically, we condemn ourselves to a self-made purgatory. Nor is this a journey we make only once. Rather it is a lifelong commitment to live honestly with ourselves and transparent before the Lord.

It is worth all the effort, though, for the rewards are blessed indeed. They are numerous — personal wholeness, spiritual maturity, fulfilling relationships and meaningfulness — yet none is more blessed than the depth of fellowship we experience with the Lord Himself. M. Basil Pennington calls it ". . .the experience of God, *hitlahavut,* the going out of self, the 'taste and see how good God is,' that engenders a joy that seems to belong to another realm."[3]

He goes on to say, "The peak moments of ecstasy will be few and brief, but the memory of them abides, and something deep within us says that all the strivings of life are worthwhile because of them."[4]

Endnotes

[1]Teilhard de Chardin, "The Divine Milieu," quoted in *Rebuilding Your Broken World,* pp. 86,87.

[2]Bob Benson and Michael W. Benson, *Disciplines for the Inner Life* (Waco: Word Books, 1985), p. 224.

[3]M. Basil Pennington, *A Place Apart,* quoted in *Disciplines for the Inner Life,* p. 328.

[4]Ibid.

Part II

INWARDNESS

"If you wish to live richly, deeply and spiritually you must cultivate the 'world within.' It is a thrilling world...with the Heavenly Father as our companion...."[1]

— John T. Benson, Jr.
The Nashville Tennessean

"The inward journey is an exercise, something that is cultivated; it requires concentration and attentiveness. Above all, the inward journey requires the greatest sincerity of which we are capable. It entails a risk — the risk of shame if nothing is there, the risk of emptiness if one does not change as a result, the risk of one's own person — and this risk is no less than that encountered on the way to another person. For us moderns, perhaps, fear of being ridiculous in our own eyes is the greatest shame."[2]

— Dorothee Soelle
Death by Bread Alone

Part II

INWARDNESS

It has been pointed out that our lives are generally made up of three components. First, there is the vocational: a person's career. Second, there is the relational: one's interaction with significant others — spouse, children, parents and peers. Third, there's the realm of inwardness: the part of a person's self that is genuinely unique and which is expressed simply for his or her private delight. And I believe there is a fourth component: the spiritual — one's relationship with God.

In this part, we turn our attention to the realm of inwardness, self-knowledge. I agree with Alexander Whyte who wrote: "To know myself, and especially as the wise man says, to know the plague of my own heart, is the true and the only key to all other true knowledge: God and man; the Redeemer and the devil; heaven and hell; faith, hope, and charity; unbelief, despair, and malignity, and all things of that kind...; *all knowledge will come to the man who knows himself,* and to that man alone."[3] (emphasis mine)

We will begin by considering a strategy for developing this inward realm, some steps to self-knowledge, if you please. Some of the more obvious ones are: memory, introspection, journaling and covenant relationships.

Each of us is a composite of his experiences; therefore, much self-understanding can be gained by examining our memories and learning how they interact with the present. Another critical strategy is introspection — the practice of observing and analyzing one's self. Journaling, then, is the discipline of putting these God-given insights, gained through memory and introspection, into written form. Often we have only the vaguest understanding of an experience or situation until we discipline ourselves to write it down. Once we put pen to paper, our elusive thoughts seem to crystalize.

Madeleine L'Engle describes the importance of journaling for her personality when she writes:

"If I can write things out I can see them, and they are not trapped within my own subjectivity. . . .

"Not long ago someone I love said something which wounded me grievously, and I was desolate that this person could have made such a comment to me.

"So, in great pain, I crawled to my journal and wrote it all out in a great burst of self-pity. And when I had set it down, when I had it before me, I saw that something I myself had said had called forth the words which had hurt me so. It had, in fact, been my own fault. But I would never have seen it if I had not written it out."[4]

And, finally, there is the holy power of covenant relationships in which we make ourselves accountable to a trusted brother or sister, and he or she to us. In this relationship, we can share our inward journey and receive the benefit of the other person's input. As Tilden Edwards observed in *Living Simply Through the Day*, "When someone else knows and cares, then we pay that much more attention to what we're doing."[5]

Developing the inward realm is demanding indeed. I'll be the first to acknowledge that. It doesn't just happen. It takes determined effort. Yet the rewards more than justify the investment of time and energy. They include (but are not limited to) inner peace, self-understanding, and an appreciation and understanding of others which leads to meaningful relationships. The final benefit is a fulfilling spiritual life.

When we are young, it has been observed, we tend to over-invest in one area of our lives at the expense of all the other areas. A man generally throws himself into his work — and with good cause, it can be argued. Not only is the marketplace competitive, but a man usually starts out in an entry-level position, knowing that all hope of career advancement depends on his performance. Add to that situation the burden of providing for the family, and it's not hard to see why a man invests so much time and energy in his career. As a result, he usually has limited understanding of himself and can relate to others only on the most superficial level. He "does" things with his friends — they play golf or tennis, go fishing or hunting, etc. — but they don't really "know" each other.

His wife, on the other hand, is often involved in making a home and caring for the children. Even when she works outside the home, it is still the woman who usually provides the majority of nurture for the family, especially

111

for the children. As a consequence, she really doesn't have any more opportunity than her husband for developing the inward realm. She's more relational than he is, but not necessarily more in touch with her inward realm. She invests in others, especially her family, at the expense of the development of her own self-knowledge.

Tragically, the Church, with its emphasis on doing rather than becoming, also contributes to the demands which make it seem almost impossible to find time for development of self-knowledge. Add the widespread ignorance which surrounds this subject, and you can see why so few of us really pursue this area of our lives.

Having said all of that, let me hasten to add that none of this will make us immune to the consequences of our imbalance. If we hope to escape the dearth that characterizes life for so many, we must accept the responsibility for making an appropriate investment of ourselves in all the areas of our lives, including the inward realm.

Endnotes

[1]John T. Benson, Jr., *The Nashville Tennessean,* published in the mid-1940's, quoted in *Disciplines for the Inner Life* by Bob Benson and Michael W. Benson (Waco: Word Books, 1985).

[2]Dorothee Soelle, *Death by Bread Alone,* quoted in *Disciplines for the Inner Life,* p. 10.

[3]Alexander Whyte, "Bunyan's Characters," quoted in *Rebuilding Your Broken World* by Gordon MacDonald (Nashville: Oliver Nelson, A Division of Thomas Nelson Publishers, 1988), p. 75.

[4]Madeleine L'Engle, reprint from *Walking On Water: Reflections on Faith and Art* (Wheaton, Illinois: Harold Shaw Publishers, copyright © Crosswicks 1980). Used by permission of Harold Shaw Publishers.

[5]Tilden H. Edwards, *Living Simply Through the Day,* quoted in *Disciplines for the Inner Life,* p. 104.

Chapter 9

THE INWARD JOURNEY
"Exploring Our Past"

Very few of us are really in touch with our inner realm. We recognize the reflection in the mirror, but in truth we are strangers to ourselves. We know the date of our birth, the color of our eyes, the tint of our hair, the day we were married, but, beyond these superficial facts, who are we really?

Most of us live on "auto-pilot." We accept our feelings, at face value, without examining them, without making any effort to determine either their origin or their validity. Or else we repress them, deny their existence. Seldom, if ever, do we examine ourselves. We act and react, laugh and cry, love one another and betray one another, without ever pausing to determine why we do the things we do. *Sumus quod sumus* — we are what we are.

As a consequence, we lead lives of carefully camouflaged loneliness. If we have mastered the social graces and are gregarious by nature, we may appear to be happy, but on the inside we are strangely unfulfilled. In unguarded moments we catch ourselves wondering if this is all there is to life. To compensate we usually maintain a hectic schedule. Anything, even exhaustion, is better than the gnawing emptiness which overtakes us if ever we pause in our mad rush through life.

Those among us less skilled at the superficial art of social convenience are even more vulnerable. Lacking the whirl of activity and the facade of friendship, such people frequently find themselves alone and forced to deal with depression and self-doubt. Unfortunately, they seldom use their "aloneness" to get acquainted with themselves or God. Not infrequently they become victims of a perpetual self-pity or addicts of the inane offerings of television.

Even those who are apparently well-adjusted and happy often lack a true understanding of themselves and those closest to them. They are interesting conversationalists, but the things they talk about are mostly secondary matters, trivial and external to themselves. The matters that are really essential, intimate, personal, are never mentioned, and likely not even understood. In truth, there is only a superficial exchange of information. And while these people appear genuinely happy, it is doubtful that they know the depth of relationship or the meaningfulness of life that God intends for them.

Such meaningfulness and spiritual depth can be experienced only as a person allows the Holy Spirit to make known unto him his true self, the inner man. Since his true self is a composite of his God-given uniqueness, his heredity, and his life experiences, this self-knowledge can only come as he examines his memories and how he relates to God and others. To obtain the necessary objectivity, he must have a trusted friend or companion with whom he can share his deepest feelings and most real memories. That friend, in turn, reflects and interprets those experiences back to him. Of course, all of this must be done in the light of God's Word and by the power of the Holy Spirit.

In *To Understand Each Other*, Dr. Paul Tournier, the eminent Swiss psychiatrist and beloved Christian, explains the importance of sharing our memories. He writes: "No one can develop freely in this world and find a full life without feeling understood by at least one person. Misunderstood, he loses his self-confidence, he loses his faith in life or even in God. He is blocked and he regresses."[1]

And to be understood, the importance of his past must be grasped. Tournier goes on to say, ". . . It is thus vain to hope to understand (him). . .without listening long, and with great interest, to his childhood and adolescent stories."[2]

In this sense, he believes it is ". . . imperative, in fact, that all of us in some fashion, become psychotherapists for one another.

"The essential part of psychotherapy is listening, long and passionate listening, with love and respect and with a real effort at understanding. It is the effort to go beyond the apparent and to discover the hidden or distant causation. This is the daily experience of psychologists. They hear a man tell his life story, in a hasty manner at first, simplified and laid out something like a biographical data sheet. It is not possible yet to understand very much in such a too-schematized account. But we must not interrupt him. It is after he has said all that seemed important to him that other memories, more emotionally charged, will come to his mind. Often these are incidents of such little apparent importance that he would not have thought of telling them had he not been encouraged by the complete attention with which we listen to him.

"Thus, bit by bit, he discovers the importance of these incidents. Now we can understand him because he is beginning to understand himself better. He realizes the importance of his very first childhood impressions, of the way in which he became conscious of himself and of the world around him. He recalls his first relationships with his parents, each of them, then with his brothers and sisters and with others who gradually entered into his world. Modern psychology has taught us the decisive role played by our earliest experiences. Our lifelong attitudes to others were determined by them. Many of these events we have forgotten. It is by talking about them that reminiscences come, or even dreams which present them to us in veiled symbolism."[3]

I once ministered to a tragically tormented young woman. Although she was strikingly attractive and gifted, she lived with an overwhelming sense of worthlessness. It permeated her personality, colored her perception of life and undermined all of her relationships. The root cause of this deeply ingrained feeling, and all the tragedies it birthed — three divorces, psychiatric treatment in a state hospital, and several suicide attempts — was a haunting childhood memory.

She remembered her parents arguing loudly. They were living on a military base in Korea, and the angry words ricocheted off the bare walls of their drab apartment, terrifying her. As she huddled in the corner whimpering, her father suddenly turned, grabbed her, and ran out of the house and across an open field.

A road bordered the field and when he reached it, he stopped. As he stood there gasping for breath, trembling violently, a heavy troop truck topped the hill and descended toward them. When it drew abreast, he raised her above his head and, with an insane scream, flung her into its pathway.

Miraculously, the huge truck wheels missed her, and her physical injuries were not serious. Emotionally, though, she was crippled for life. The sight of the huge truck's ugly underside became a haunting memory, inhabiting her thoughts by day and her dreams by night. It tormented her, constantly reminding her that she was unloved and unwanted.

Once she was able to share the memory of that experience, it was not too difficult to help her see how it had affected all the relationships of her life. If her own father did not love her, did not want her — if, in fact, he had attempted to kill her — then she must be worthless, or so her twisted reasoning went. As a consequence, she unconsciously sought out and built relationships with men who were themselves wounded and incapable of maintaining a relationship, thus making further rejection almost inevitable. She was the victim of a self-fulfilling prophecy, and her own distrust only hastened the preordained end. Each broken relationship simply reinforced her warped self-image.

This young woman's case is an extreme example, I'll grant you, but it does serve to illustrate the part our past plays in our personalities and our relationships. By examining our memories we can begin to understand ourselves better, and thus bring our "real" selves to God for healing and forgiveness. It's only as we "own" our past (that is, recall and accept all that has happened to us, and all that we have done) that God's grace can truly make us new. That which we deny or repress is beyond the reach of His grace, and thus lives on to torment us and undermine our relationships.

We see a beautiful example of this kind of emotional healing in Jesus' ministry to the woman at the well. (John 4:3-42.) Although John does not see fit to provide us with the specific details of this woman's past, it is obvious that she, too, is tormented by painful memories and personal failure. And, like most of us, she has learned to live a lie, to repress that which she cannot bear to remember, to pretend to be something she is not. Therefore, when Jesus tells her to go and call her husband, she replies, "I have no husband." (John 4:17.)

"Jesus said to her, 'You are right when you say you have no husband. The fact is, you have had five husbands, and the man you now have is not your husband. What you have just said is quite true.'

"'Sir,' the woman said, 'I can see that you are a prophet....'

"Then, leaving her water jar, the woman went back to the town and said to the people, 'Come, see a man who told me everything I ever did. Could this be the Christ?'"

John 4:18,19,28,29

As I was studying this passage, I began to realize, maybe for the first time, the significance of allowing Jesus to make our real selves known to us, even as He confronted the Samaritan woman with the truth about herself. Although it is potentially a frightening experience, it is also liberating. Freed from the need to pretend to be someone she wasn't, she could finally come to grips with herself. She could finally accept the truth about herself, the truth which heretofore had been simply too terrible to face. And there, in the presence of Jesus, she found love which accepted her as she was, and, at the same time, a redeeming love that released her from her shameful past.

Then I prayed:

"Lord,
all of us
are a little like
the Samaritan woman at the well.
We have sins and failure in our past,
a closet full of skeletons
which rattle from time to time,
threatening to get out
and spoil our good image.
For many of us
it's not just skeletons either,
but real live boogie men.

"For the most part
we keep them tightly suppressed,
but from time to time they escape,
terrorizing our families,
and reducing us to guilt and confusion.
I hate and fear
the boogie man inside of me.
The egomaniac
who talks too much.

119

The proud presumptuous me.
The critical, cutting me.
The carnal man,
my feet of clay.
The pseudo-spiritual me.

"The Samaritan woman
found release
when You told her
everything she had done.
Does this mean
blackmailing boogie men
cannot survive
in the light of Your
loving acceptance?
If it does,
then tell me,
tell us,
everything we've ever done.
Show us the futility of pretending
and protesting our innocence.
Give us the courage
to own up,
and in this owning up,
let us find forgiveness and freedom.

"Amen."

That's the real challenge for many of us — to allow
the Lord to tell us everything we have done. The average
person has repressed much of his past, especially that which
is painful. And all of us have things of which we are
ashamed. "Things in our past" that, according to Tournier,
"we should like to blot out, things for which we feel ourselves

responsible."[4] Yet our only hope, our only path to freedom, is honest confession.

It isn't only painful memories which shape our personality, which make us who we are, but all memories. For instance, my love for kerosene lamps and quiet talks undoubtedly comes from my memory of long winter evenings spent in deep conversation with my Grandma Miller. Around us the tiny living room glowed in the soft warmth of yellow light spilling from a solitary kerosene lamp.

My dad has always been an avid reader, and when I was just a baby I would sit on his lap for hours, perfectly still, while he read. Thinking about that now, I realize that my own love for books may well have been born right there in his arms. Even today I think of a good book as a trusted friend, and I associate them with happiness and love. Is it not possible that those warm feelings are a carryover of the love and security I found in my father's arms?

I have a natural love for and trust in people, which I believe comes from the security of my childhood. My family didn't have a lot of material possessions, but our home was rich in love and laughter. Never can I recall doubting my parents' love for me. I still get a warm feeling when I remember Dad standing on the sidelines, night after night, watching me practice junior high football. And Mother always had a hot supper ready for me when I came in at 9:30 from my after-school job. The memory of our late-evening talks while I ate are special to me still, these many years later. In times of great disappointment and personal failure, the strength of those memories, and the relationships they symbolize, has sustained me.

121

Put your finger between the pages now and take a few minutes to reflect on your own life. Begin with a positive memory. Let the warm feelings of love and acceptance wash over you. Luxuriate in yesterday's joys and the deep relationships which nurtured and shaped you. Explore the ways those past experiences have formed your values and influenced the decisions which have guided your life. Now remember some significant spiritual experiences, some times when God made Himself especially real to you. Relive a critical moment in your life when His faithfulness sustained and strengthened you as nothing else could. See how that too has shaped the faith by which you now live.

Perhaps your memories are painful, more like those of the young woman to whom I ministered who had been rejected by her parents, especially her father. Even now you feel an aching emptiness rather than a comforting warmth. Your past seems like a nuclear winter, desolate and frozen. Don't turn away! As painful as it may be, that too is who you are. Deny it, and you deny a part of yourself. Repress it, and you sentence yourself to a lifetime of irrational responses and misdirected outbursts. Embrace it. Feel the pain. Shed the tears you have so long withheld. You are not alone. Jesus is with you, and He will redeem your past (that is, make it contribute to your ultimate Christlikeness).

Dr. Tournier describes such an experience in his own life: "I lost my father when I was three months old. That is to say, I never mourned him; I was not conscious of how greatly this loss had marked my life with frustration. Well I remember the day when, after a long talk with my wife in which we really sensed the presence of God, suddenly I broke out sobbing. I got rid of an emotional charge which had been for so long a time repressed. I did not then realize, nor did she, that my wife had that day played the part of a psychotherapist. This was going to open to me just such a career."[5]

The tragedy that had haunted him his whole life long, the loss that had weighed him down and burdened him, was in that moment of honest confession transformed into a liberating and life-changing experience. Now both the pain of his loss and the joy of his release were available to God. And God used them to make Tournier one of the most effective and beloved Christian counselors in the history of the Church. Only eternity will reveal the full extent of his influence. And to think it might have all been lost had he not risked owning and sharing that painful experience.

Endnotes

[1]Paul Tournier, *To Understand Each Other,* translated by John S. Gilmour (Richmond: John Knox Press, 1962), p. 29. Copyright © 1967 M.E. Bratcher. Used by permission of Westminster/John Knox Press.

[2]Ibid., p. 51.

[3]Ibid., pp. 50,51.

[4]Ibid., p. 53.

[5]Ibid., p. 52.

Chapter 10

THE KEY TO UNDERSTANDING YOURSELF

"Examine Our Relationships"

The Holy Spirit guides us to examine not only our past, but our present as well. We learn much about ourselves by prayerfully contemplating our relationships, the way we interact with people. These too reflect the character of our inner man, just as light and heat are manifestations of fire. In the crucible of interpersonal relationships, the nature of a man's heart is made known. In moments of pressure or confrontation, his true self is revealed. Unfortunately, we often excuse these inappropriate displays without examining their roots, or we blame them on the other person. We would do well to remember that Jesus said: "...out of the overflow of the heart the mouth speaks. The good man brings good things out of the good stored up in him, and the evil man brings evil things out of the evil stored up in him" (Matt. 12:34,35).

Years ago I served on a board with a man who was a classic example of this very thing. I recall more than one occasion on which he closed his briefcase and stormed out of a meeting. He was well-educated, successful and articulate, but he was a tormented man, and the slightest rejection, imagined or real, would set him off. I realized, as I'm sure the other board members did too, that he was reacting to something more than the current agenda. The problem was — he didn't realize it. In his mind his response was appropriate, and we were to blame for the breakdown in board relationships.

Unfortunately, he is not alone. The world is full of people just like him. People whose emotional responses are disproportionate to the events that trigger them. Such outbursts, however, can be redemptive if they are carefully examined, if the person will ask the Holy Spirit to show him why such insignificant issues generate so much emotion. Tragically, few people are willing to invest the necessary time and energy. As a result, they condemn themselves and those they love to years of frustration and embarrassing behavior.

It may be good at this point to differentiate between honesty and transparency. When a person is honest, he expresses his true feelings about a given issue or situation. A transparent person, on the other hand, focuses on himself rather than the event or circumstance. He shares what God is showing him about himself through that experience. The aforementioned man was very honest, but he was not at all transparent. He told us exactly how he felt, but he never shared his inner struggles or how he arrived at his conclusions. Both honesty and transparency are critical to healthy and productive relationships.

How, you may be wondering, does a person go about developing this kind of self-understanding? First, he must make a commitment, he must see it as a spiritual discipline necessary if he hopes to experience personal growth and wholeness. If he sees it as anything else, then it becomes optional. Next, he must set aside time on a regular basis (daily is best) to wait before the Lord. He should present the circumstances and relationships of his life to the Lord for examination, being sensitive to the thoughts and impressions he receives. These are often insights from the Lord.

Personally, I find it most effective to use a prayer journal. By disciplining myself to write out my thoughts and feelings in detail, I am better able to understand them, better able to see them in a more objective light. For instance, some years ago I was having difficulty with a staff member and I found myself dealing with a lot of anger. In an attempt to get things into perspective, I wrote:

"Lord,
I've had to deal with anger a lot over the years.
And I've used a variety of strategies —
    I've suffered in silence and grown bitter.
    I've lashed out in retaliation and lived to regret it.
    I've tried to give in and ended up feeling used and trapped.

I've confronted in love, tough love, and grieved
as I was misunderstood and feared.
Is there any good way of dealing with anger?
    Quickly, before it gets dug in,
        before it becomes a part of one's psyche?
    Confession to God...
        forgiveness of the perpetrator?
"Still, Lord,
there must be a better way.
An attitude,
    a way of looking at things,
        which nips it in the bud.
For me, it means knowing when to give in...graciously...
    and knowing what things are mine to give.
For me, it means standing firm...up front...
    when the issue is non-negotiable.
I cannot hope it will "work itself out."
I cannot need the approval of my colleagues so much
    that I am unable to take a stand.
When I postpone dealing with an issue I hurt everyone
        involved.
    Anger hangs thick and heavy between us
    and by the time we deal with it,
it has become a monster raging out of control.
"Sanctify me, Lord.
Let me freely yield that which is mine to yield.
Show me,
    help me to know,
what is Yours to guard
    and what is mine to give.
In Christ's name, I pray.

"Amen."

Through that experience, and several others in which I've found myself wrestling with varying degrees of anger, I am learning much about the kind of person I really am. Some of it is painful and unflattering. For instance, some of my anger is the product of little hurts, carefully kept for years, which suddenly explode in the most inappropriate ways. The issue that finally triggers it is usually a legitimate concern, but it is soon lost in the outpouring of my emotion.

To combat this destructive tendency, I am keeping shorter accounts with God and with others. If someone hurts me, I now do my best to deal with that situation posthaste. Sometimes this simply means taking it to the Lord and realizing that the fault is mine. Once I understand the true cause, I can receive God's forgiveness and be done with it. If after prayer I still feel that the other person is at fault, I then choose to forgive him in God's presence. That means I let go of the hurt and the anger.

If the person who wounded me is a colleague or close friend, then I must take an additional step. I must go to him (in love, not anger) and work out our differences. If the offending person is simply an acquaintance, someone whom I see only occasionally, then I may forego the second step, but only if he is unaware of my feelings toward him. Since I have already forgiven him, there is nothing between us, my anger is gone.

I could continue with other incidents from my own life and journal, but I think the point is well taken. Let me hasten to add, though, that journaling is a key tool in self-understanding and personal spiritual growth. It is neither a recent discovery nor the invention of believers with a psychological bent. Journaling is a historical spiritual discipline. In fact, the keeping of personal journals has played a significant role in the history of the Church, particularly where the value of the inner life is taken seriously. From St. Augustine to Pascal to the Society of Friends, some form of the spiritual journal has been used for spiritual discipline and growth.

Elizabeth O'Conner writes in *Letters to Scattered Pilgrims:* "Among our primary tools for growth are reflection, self-observation and self-questioning. The journal is one of the most helpful vehicles we have for cultivating these great powers in ourselves. *We all have these powers but we need structures that encourage us to use and practice them. Journal writing is enforced reflection.* When we commit our observations to writing we are taking what is inside us and placing it outside us. We are holding a piece of our life in our hands where we can look at it, and meditate on it, and deepen our understanding of it."[1] (emphasis mine)

In the introduction to his practical little volume on journaling, Robert Wood writes: "Keeping a journal is the process of digesting the spiritual meaning of the events of each day. These events have come with rapidity; they have come with feeling, some with thinking, some with just doing. Sometime during your hurried day you must take time out to reflect on the deeper significance of these events and to digest them into your own 'life-sustaining milk.' As you make sense of them, you will put them in perspective of their importance and lasting value to your own life."[2]

Yet as significant as journaling is, it is not enough. The inward journey to self-understanding and transparency will never be experienced in its full dimensions until it includes a covenant relationship of mutual accountability. Each person needs a friend or friends with whom he can share his deepest stirrings, his most profound discoveries, and receive in return sincere and loving reflections. Not infrequently the observations of others provide the necessary piece which completes the picture and enables the person to truly see himself as God sees him. Additionally, the knowledge that at least one other individual knows him as he really is helps him to resist the temptation to fall back into his self-deceptive lifestyle.

Paul Tournier contends that ". . . no one comes to know himself through introspection, or in the solitude of his personal diary. Rather, it is in dialogue, in his meeting with other persons. It is only by expressing his conviction to others that he becomes really conscious of them. He who would see himself clearly must open up to a confidant freely chosen and worthy of such trust. It may be a friend just as easily as a doctor; it may also be one's marital partner."[3]

His emphasis on covenant relationships of mutual accountability should not be understood as minimizing the importance of journaling. Rather, they should be considered equally important, as both play a vital role in the development of self-understanding, emotional wholeness and spiritual maturity.

Gordon MacDonald, past president of InterVarsity Christian Fellowship and author of several best-selling books, including *Ordering Your Private World,* writes about the absolute necessity of mutual accountability. He speaks not only from a pastoral perspective, but as one who has experienced the tragic consequences which often come when one ignores this vital area. Following his public confession of a past moral failure, he explained, but did not excuse, his behavior in an interview with *Christianity Today*.[4]

According to MacDonald, one of the contributing factors was a lack of mutual accountability through personal relationships: friendships in which one man regularly looks another man in the eyes and asks hard questions about his moral life, his lust, his ambitions, his ego.

He enlarges on this theme in his latest book, *Rebuilding Your Broken World:* "I am often asked what sort of things friends in accountability might ask of one another. Having found little if any helpful literature on this subject, I put together a list of twenty-six questions...

1. How is your relationship with God right now?
2. What have you read in the Bible in the past week?
3. What has God said to you in this reading?
4. Where do you find yourself resisting Him these days?
5. What specific things are you praying for in regard to others?
6. What specific things are you praying for in regard to yourself?
7. What are the specific tasks facing you right now that you consider incomplete?
8. What habits intimidate you?
9. What have you read in the secular press this week?
10. What general reading are you doing?
11. What have you done to play?
12. How are you doing with your spouse? Kids?
13. If I were to ask your spouse about your state of mind, state of spirit, state of energy level, what would the response be?

14. Are you sensing any spiritual attacks from the enemy right now?

15. If Satan were to try to invalidate you as a person or as a servant of the Lord, how might he do it?

16. What is the state of your sexual perspective? Tempted? Dealing with fantasies? Entertainment?

17. Where are you financially right now? (things under control? under anxiety? in great debt?)

18. Are there any unresolved conflicts in your circle of relationships right now?

19. When was the last time you spent time with a good friend of your own gender?

20. What kind of time have you spent with anyone who is a non-Christian this past month?

21. What challenges do you think you're going to face in the coming week? Month?

22. What would you say are your fears at this present time?

23. Are you sleeping well?

24. What three things are you most thankful for?

25. Do you like yourself at this point in your pilgrimage?

26. What are your greatest confusions about your relationship with God?"[5]

Holding another person accountable is a special responsibility, and no one can take that responsibility upon himself. It is something that is grown even more than given. Through the process of time and friendship, a bond of love and trust is developed. Little by little each one reveals more and more about himself, and as each revelation is treated with respect, trust is deepened. After a time there comes

133

a certain safety in the relationship, and mutual account-ability simply evolves. Because you care about each other, you share honestly and lovingly.

Once another person grants you that degree of trust, you must treat it with absolute respect. You now have tremendous power for good or for evil. Used with loving discretion, it can be an instrument which facilitates spiritual growth. In the hands of the wrong person, it can be used to manipulate and control. I'm not trying to discourage you from this God-given task, but I feel we must fully understand the risks before we can appreciate the awesome weight of the responsibility involved.

As I endeavor to live out several relationships of mutual accountability, I recognize with increasing frequency my own shortcomings. More often than I care to admit, I have failed those who depended upon me. Still, I cannot give up. I cannot retreat into the pseudo-safety of superficial relationships. I must continue, for it is only in the doing that I develop the skills to be a true friend. With simple sincerity I ask God to make me the kind of friend I should be. With His help I believe I can strengthen and encourage those I love.

And when I do fail, I believe He can redeem my failures. I often find myself praying with Norman B. Nash: "O God, you have made us for fellowship, and have given us the power both to help and harm our fellows, grant us the wisdom to know what is their good, and the ready will to help them to attain it. Heal those we have wounded, strengthen those whom we have failed, grant us all your healing grace, and make our fellowship to be your family, through Jesus Christ our Lord, Amen."[6]

Endnotes

[1]Elizabeth O'Conner, *Letters to Scattered Pilgrims,* quoted in *Disciplines for the Inner Life* by Bob Benson and Michael W. Benson (Waco: Word Books, 1985), p. 100.

[2]From *A Thirty-day Experiment In Prayer* by Robert Woods. Copyright © 1978 by *The Upper Room*, 1908 Grand Avenue, P. O. Box 189, Nashville, TN 37202. Used by permission of the publisher.

[3]Tournier, p. 30.

[4]"A Talk with the MacDonalds," *Christianity Today,* July 10, 1987, p. 39.

[5]Gordon MacDonald, *Rebuilding Your Broken World* (Nashville: Oliver Nelson, A Division of Thomas Nelson Publishers, 1988), pp. 203,204.

[6]Norman B. Nash, *Daily Prayer Companion,* quoted in *Disciplines for the Inner Life,* p. 103.

Chapter 11

FACING THE TRUTH ABOUT OURSELVES

It is impossible to give serious consideration to the inward journey without realizing that the disciplines involved are demanding indeed. Add to this the risks — the loss of our carefully constructed self-image, the way we are perceived by the public, and the very real possibility that we will be misunderstood — and it becomes obvious why so few of us are really willing to commit ourselves to it. The fact that it's mandatory for our full spiritual development is true enough, but recognition of this truth is seldom sufficient to move us off of dead center. In order to make the kind of commitment required by the inward journey, we must also be fully convinced of its benefits.

The personal benefits include self-understanding, emotional wholeness and inner peace. Add to these the benefit of enhanced relationships. Once a person experiences inner peace, and a degree of self-understanding, he is better prepared to develop meaningful relationships. Because he is whole, he is now attracted to others who share a like wholeness, thus improving his possibilities of establishing healthy and fulfilling relationships. And, finally, there is the benefit of a deeper spiritual life — a life based on being and becoming, rather than simply doing and achieving; on intimacy with God, rather than "busyness" for God.

In a previous chapter, I alluded briefly to our Lord's ministry to the woman at the well. Like many of us, she is a person with a flawed past. She has secret sins and hidden failures, things she would rather not discuss. And, like us, she soon learns that, while she may deny them, she cannot escape them. Their persistent painfulness is always just below the surface, and it only takes a knowing glance, or a telling word, to bring it all back. Thus when Jesus tells her to go and call her husband, she becomes instantly defensive. Curtly, she informs Him that she has no husband.

Although John's recording of this poignant passage is brief, it is packed with profound implications. In this woman's tragic history we see much of our own. Not necessarily the marital failure and immorality, but the duplicity and self-deception. She is ashamed of her past; she wishes she could go back and change it, but she can't. Instead, she practices a determined denial. If she doesn't think about it, if she pretends it didn't happen, then perhaps she can escape its painfulness.

Unfortunately, denial is no more effective for her than it is for us. Instead of escaping her disastrous past, she is condemned to live always with its ever-present shadow. Even when she establishes a new relationship, one in which her past is not known, she lives in constant fear of being found out. Thus, she has to work all the harder to convince others that she really is the person they perceive her to be.

It isn't hard to imagine her inner turmoil. She wants to be different, but she doubts that she ever will be. She longs for meaningful friendships, but is afraid to let anyone know her. She is quite convinced that if they knew her as she is really is, they would reject her. Yet relationships built on falsehood are exhausting and unfulfilling. Is there any hope for her, for us? Yes, but only if we can "come clean" with ourselves and with God!

"Studies suggest that more than half of American midlife males live with at least one secret in the past of their personal lives, and these men believe its revelation would bring about catastrophic consequences for them and those close to them."[1] These studies only confirm what I've long suspected. And they simply reinforce the dire need for the kind of ministry Jesus brought to this desperately lonely woman.

Her salvation, and ours, lies in letting Him comfort us with the truth about ourselves. Following her curt denial of having a husband, "Jesus said to her, 'You are right when you say you have no husband. The fact is, you have had five husbands, and the man you now have is not your husband...'" (John 4:17,18).

That revelation was both terrifying and liberating. Terrifying, because now He may reject her, or worse yet, use her like the rest. Liberating, because she is free from the burden of pretending, free from the fear of being found out. Since Jesus already knows all about her, she can be herself. And soon her fear gives way to joyous wonder. He does not reject her, nor does He use her, rather He forgives and transforms her!

"Then, leaving her water jar, the woman went back to the town and said to the people, *'Come, see a man who told me everything I ever did.* Could this be the Christ?'" (John 4:28,29). (emphasis mine)

For the first time in longer than she can remember, she is at peace. The inner enemies of weakness and habit have been defeated, the accusing voices strangely stilled. In their place is a quiet assurance. She is loved. She is accepted. The past cannot torment her, for she is forgiven. It cannot blackmail her, for it has been exposed to the light of His loving acceptance. The future is no longer foreboding, for she is a new person. Together with God she can make her life what He intends it to be.

Such inner harmony is possible only for those who have made peace with themselves. As long as a person denies his past, as long as he tries to ignore the turbulent emotions struggling within, he condemns himself to a debilitating inner discord. With supreme self-discipline he may be able to function in a socially acceptable manner, but on the inside he is miserable.

Victims of abuse or incest are a classic example. Few experiences in life are more devastating. Those who have gone through this trauma often live with feelings of absolute worthlessness. As unreasonable as it may seem, almost every victim feels responsible, as if it were somehow his or her fault. Many of them live their entire lives tormented by their unspeakable secret.

In *Betrayal of Innocence*, Susan Forward writes: "Last year I met a young psychiatric nurse who admitted to me that as a child she had been raped several times by her brother and repeatedly forced by her father to perform fellatio. I asked how the experience affected her. Her reply haunts me still. 'Think of the lowest thing in the world, and whatever that is, I'm lower.'"[2]

Some years ago I had a special opportunity to minister God's healing grace to a lady who, more than thirty years after the incident, was still struggling with the aftermath of incest. One evening at church, just as I stepped to the pulpit to begin my message, the Spirit gave me an inner vision. I don't know what else to call it. Suddenly, like slides projected on the screen of my mind, I saw a series of pictures.

In the first picture I saw a stylishly dressed woman who appeared to be in her early forties. On the outside she seemed calm and collected, but on the inside she was tormented and out of control. In the second picture I saw a young girl, of six or seven, run out the screen door of a sagging frame house and onto a wooden porch. She was crying as she stumbled down the steps and ran into a wooded pasture. In the third picture I saw Jesus take her into His arms. He wiped away her tears, comforted her. Soon she was at peace.

Almost instantly I knew what those pictures meant. I described them to the congregation. Then I told them that there was a woman in the service who had been sexually molested by her uncle when she was seven years old, and that Jesus was present in a special way to heal her. Finally, I prayed a simple healing prayer.

After the meeting an attractive middle-aged woman made it a point to thank me for my ministry. When she did, she left a note in my hand. It simply said: "I was that seven-year-old girl. My father's cousin molested me and I ran from the house just as you described. I've never told anyone, though that experience has haunted me all these years. Tonight Jesus healed me. I feel like a new person."

In truth, Jesus comes to each of us in the same way. He takes "the lamp of the LORD" and steps into our private world. There, in the secret chambers of our inner lives, He confronts us with the truth about ourselves. He comes, not to embarrass or humiliate, but to deliver us from our painful past. If we have lived with secret sins, and the accompanying guilt and fear, He comes to forgive. If we have been victimized, by life or by loved ones, He comes to heal and restore. Always He comes to make us new.

Still there's something shocking about having our most carefully guarded secrets suddenly revealed, and it's not unusual to react with anger or fear. Like the woman at the well, we often protest our innocence ("I have no husband"). Or we flee in fear. But this "Hound of Heaven" will not be put off. Deeper He descends, with that dreadful lamp, exposing yet more of our subterranean world to the light of His deliverance.

And it isn't only victims of incest who have a "secret life," but a goodly portion of the Christian community. Some people are tormented by the memory of a secret abortion to get rid of a child conceived outside of marriage. Now they die a little every time someone mentions the subject. Others live with the pain of marital infidelity or substance abuse. They live in fear of the dreaded day when their hidden life will be discovered. Still others harbor secret fears, unspeakable jealousies, dishonest business dealings or outright hatred.

For many of us, though, our "secret" is not some clandestine sin as much as it is just a gross ignorance of who we really are. We have been so busy doing that we have never taken the time to develop a knowledge of self. We've perfected a number of roles — parent, child, husband, father, wife, mother, employee, business associate, church member, public servant — but we've never learned to be ourselves. We do things with people, but we find it impossible to relate to them on a personal basis. As a consequence, our relationships are superficial and unfulfilling, even with the people closest to us.

Some years ago Jesus began dealing with me about this very issue in my own life. After spending all of my adult life in the ministry, with its multiple roles and expectations, I had lost touch with myself. I had spent so many years trying to be what people expected me to be that I no longer knew who I really was. Although I had numerous acquaintances, although I knew the deepest secrets of many counselees, I was not intimate with anyone.

In desperation I prayed:

"Lord,
If intimacy is
knowing and being known,
how can I ever be intimate?
I mean,
how can I let someone else know me
when I don't even know myself?
Being me
is a role I've never quite managed.

"I read people,
like an amateur actor reads cue cards.
Their expectations script my life.
Do they expect me to be funny?
Then I'll don my clown face
and smoke them with laughter.
If it's a sensitive man they want,
I'll put on my listening face.
I'll furrow my brow in concentration.
I'll grimace in pain,
sigh when I'm supposed to.

"I'm the same way with You, Lord.
I'm afraid to be myself,
afraid to let You see me
as I really am.
I study others,
memorize how they act around You.
I've got it down pretty well too;
but it isn't me.
It isn't real!
It's safe.
Nobody ever gets hurt,
but it's empty and lonely,
and I don't think I can
manage it much longer.
Do I dare ask You
to reveal Yourself to me,
to reveal my true self to me?

"I take the chance, Lord.
With halting speech I pray,
'Know me, O Lord,
know my heart and my thoughts,

know my secret self,
the part that's a stranger even to me.'

"With tentative hands
I fumble with my masks.
I've worn them so long
they seem to be a part of me.
With determined persistence I pull,
I tug until at last they come off.
I'm not sure I like what I see,
but at least I'm face to face with me.
We shake hands,
the empty man I used to be,
and me.
We merge,
become one,
and at last I'm free.
Free to know
and to be known.
Free to be intimate.
Free to be me.
Thanks, Lord,
I couldn't have done it alone.

"Amen."

My relationships didn't instantly change, but my perception of them did. I realized that I couldn't be intimate friends with everyone. There simply wasn't enough time or emotional energy. But I determined to strive to be emotionally present, to be "real" each time I interacted with someone. And I began to get in touch with myself. I came to recognize my own emotional needs as legitimate and to seek spiritually valid ways to meet them. I started spending more "real" time with Brenda. Before, I had been conscientious about fulfilling my duties as a Christian husband and father, but now I became emotionally involved as well. I made a commitment to know her and to understand her as a unique person of special worth.

Slowly I began to change, and as I did the significant relationships of my life started to deepen and mature. Now, several years later, I can look back on that experience (in which Jesus showed me the emptiness of my inner life) and rejoice. As painful as it was, as demanding as the changes have been, it was the most blessed thing that ever happened to me.

It isn't over yet, and probably never will be. I face a constant battle to maintain integrity in my inner life and relationships. If I relax for a minute, I find myself slipping back into the old habit of role-playing instead of relating honestly. When this happens, I simply repent and recommit myself to the task at hand. And I thank God that I can now recognize the difference and do something about it before I find myself trapped again in a desert of busy but unfulfilling relationships.

Endnotes

[1]Gordon MacDonald, *Rebuilding Your Broken World* (Nashville: Oliver Nelson, A Division of Thomas Nelson Publishers, 1988), p. 72.

[2]Susan Forward and Craig Buck, *Betrayal of Innocence,* copyright © 1978, Jeremy P. Tarcher, Inc., Los Angeles, California 90069, p. 120.

Chapter 12

FREE AT LAST

As a person allows the Lord to make his inner life known to him, he discovers that he also has a greater understanding of other people. No longer does he judge everything by outward appearances. Knowing that his own behavior is often a role, he now makes a genuine attempt to understand others. Realizing that he has often reacted to people or events based not on the current situation, but out of past disappointment, he now seeks for ways to minister rather than simply reacting. He looks behind a person's actions in an effort to discern his true intent, the source of those actions. Not in a judgmental or suspicious way, but in an attempt to truly understand.

Understanding is, in fact, the foundation for relationships. Once we understand another person, we can meet him where he is. This was the secret of Jesus' earthly

147

ministry. He understood people and met them at the point of their need.

This truth was driven home to me in my own marriage. For years I had frustrated Brenda with advice and exhortations. Whenever she shared a problem or concern with me, I always had a ready answer. The things that troubled her seemed so insignificant to me, so easy to solve. Unfortunately, it was not my "wisdom" she sought, but my understanding. Not realizing this, I continued to advise her, instead of relating to her, until she finally stopped discussing her concerns with me at all. I was a "fixer," but what she really needed was a compassionate husband who would simply accept her and listen with love.

Needless to say, my insensitivity was not without its consequences. She stopped sharing her needs and concerns, but I hardly noticed, so busy was I in my own world. My easy answers and constant advice had only made her feel silly and inadequate. And angry, I might add. So she suffered alone with her hurt. Over the years this suffering in silence, plus the never-ending demands of the ministry, took their toll, and Brenda grew depressed. She was careful to hide it from me for I had not proved worthy of her trust.

Thankfully, Jesus was doing His special work in my heart, and as I came to understand myself, I was gradually being changed, being prepared to truly be a godly husband.

One winter evening I came home early and found Brenda in the bedroom crying. When she heard my step on the stairs, she tried to dry her tears, but it was too late. With great trepidation she poured out her hurts and fears, her self-doubts. For once I listened, with compassion, and didn't try to "fix" everything. Her pain and "aloneness" became mine. I understood. Now that I had finally accepted my own needs, I could also accept hers. We sat for a long time that night, after her grief had spent itself, in loving silence.

This time there was no advice or exhortations to "do better next time." I simply loved her and accepted her in her need. On the inside I grieved, for I knew that her pain and "aloneness" was, at least partially, my fault: "If I had been more compassionate, more understanding. . . . If I had been the kind of husband I should have been. . . ." With a determined effort I refused to allow my guilt to get in the way of her need. This was Brenda's time, and I chose to be there for her.

That night was a turning point in our lives. Brenda wasn't suddenly set free of her lonely depression, but she did begin to believe that I might be able to understand her. Little by little she began to trust me with her feelings again. And, as I continued to respond with compassion and understanding, the depth of our bonding increased.

How had Tournier put it? "It is thus vain to hope to understand one's husband or wife without listening long, and with great interest. . . . The essential part. . . is listening, long and passionate listening, with love and respect and with a real effort at understanding."[1]

At last I am learning to listen. More than a little late, to be sure, but not too late, thank God! Well might Brenda have penned these words by an anonymous writer:

"When I ask you to listen to me and you start giving me advice, you have not done what I asked.

"When I ask you to listen to me and you feel you have to do something to solve my problem, you have failed me, strange as that may seem.

"Listen! All I asked was that you listen, not talk or do — just hear me.

"Advice is cheap; 20 cents will get you both 'Dear Abby' and Billy Graham in the same paper.

"I can do for myself — I'm not helpless.

"When you do something for me that I can and need to do for myself, you contribute to my fear and inadequacy.

"But when you accept as a simple fact that I do feel what I feel, no matter how irrational, then I can quit trying to convince you and get about this business of understanding what's behind this irrational feeling. When that's clear, the answers are obvious and I don't need advice.

"Non-rational feelings make more sense when we understand what's behind them.

"So please listen and just hear me.

"And if you want to talk, wait a minute for your turn — and I'll listen to you."[2]

That pretty well says it, doesn't it? Most of us are born with the ability to hear well (that is, the physical mechanism of our ear is capable of perceiving sounds and distinguishing frequencies). Unfortunately, few of us are born with the ability to listen well. It doesn't come naturally. It has to be learned.

There are a number of reasons, I suppose, why men find listening so difficult. For the most part, they are, by nature, activists, problem-solvers, take-charge personalities. It goes against the grain to simply listen. Intuitively, men feel that their manhood somehow depends on their ability to "fix" things.

Another reason a man finds it hard to truly listen is that the painful concerns being expressed often reflect the very fears he has tried so hard to deny. When his wife, or a close friend, begins to express such deep and painful anxieties, it threatens his carefully constructed denial system. The truth is, he can't really allow others to process their feelings, in his presence, until he has resolved, or at least accepted, his own.

I was able, at last, to listen to Brenda and accept her painful self-doubt because I had finally made peace with my own. I was no longer tormented by faceless fears from the unexplored depths of my inner world. With Jesus as my guide, I was exploring this inner realm, and, by the might of His Spirit, conquering the dragons which haunted those murky depths. In the past, I had been convinced that if I acknowledged my insecurities or fears, they would overwhelm me. Instead, I discovered that they couldn't long survive in the penetrating light of His lamp. And what pain remained (for in this world there will always be some pain) became a tool in His hand for the shaping of my life. He used it to carve out a well of compassion.

The Spirit was doing His holy work, and the self-knowledge it birthed produced not only an inner peace, but a compassionate understanding of others as well. And from this understanding came a renewed intimacy with my wife, and a depth and meaningfulness in my relationships that I had ceased to believe possible. This holy work continues,

151

even now, and will as long as I allow the Spirit to have His way in my life.

Endnotes

[1]Paul Tournier, *To Understand Each Other*, translated by John S. Gilmour (Richmond: John Knox Press, 1962), p. 51.

[2]Source unknown.

Part III

SIGNIFICANT OTHERS

"Some nights I am in the kitchen washing dishes and Pop is playing poker with the boys. Well, I watch him real close, and at first I'll just see an ordinary, middle-aged man, not very interesting to look at. And then, minute by minute, I'll see little things I never saw before — good things and bad things, queer little habits I never noticed he had, ways of talking I'd never paid any mind to. Suddenly I know who he is, and I love him so much I could cry and I thank God I took time to see him real."[1]

— Lizzie
The Rain Maker

Part III

SIGNIFICANT OTHERS

We are finally ready to turn our attention to the significant others in our lives, those whose presence completes us as persons and gives dimension and meaning to our lives. It is probably important to note that while we are dealing with these areas (God, inwardness, significant others and community) in succession, in real life they develop simultaneously. And while we have attempted to separate them, for the purpose of better understanding them, in truth they are interrelated and overlapping. That is to say that growth in one area quite naturally stimulates development in the other areas as well.

A tendency among us moderns is to segregate our lives (that is, to compartmentalize them). As a consequence, we often seem to be well developed in one area, while sadly lacking in some others. For instance, a man who is doing great things for God may appear to be a spiritual giant, while lacking human warmth and people skills. In truth, even his spiritual life is deficient, for it is one-dimensional. That is not to say that he is not doing "great things" for God, only that he is limiting the things God can do in him and in his relationships.

Such a person reminds me of the medieval nobleman who had a beautiful chapel in his castle. Every day he would spend time there, meditating and communing with God. Directly beneath the chapel was a torture chamber where he committed the cruelest of atrocities against his enemies. Tragically, he saw nothing incongruous in that situation. Like him, many people seem to have several levels in their lives. God appears to be very much a part of one area, while in another area their lives are blatantly un-Christian.

The challenge before us, then, is to lead integrated lives in which we experience concomitant growth, in which Jesus is Lord of all areas and of all our relationships. That is not nearly as difficult as it may sound. In fact, it happens quite naturally once we are freed from the misconceptions that have produced our segregated lives.

Concomitant growth requires that we conspicuously apply the principles of spiritual truth to all the areas of our lives. As our relationship with God deepens and matures, we must deliberately invite Him to know us, and to make our innermost selves known to us as well. As He brings truth and wholeness to these areas, we quite naturally invite Him to be Lord of our relationships, especially with those closest to us. Finally, then, He becomes Lord of our fellowship, transforming what was heretofore a loosely knit association into an extended family, a community of believers.

In this section we turn our attention to the family — our spouse and children, our parents and siblings. No relationships are more demanding. David Mace, world-renowned marriage and family counselor, writes in *Love and Anger in Marriage,* "The state of marriage generates in normal people more anger than they are likely to experience in any other type of relationship in which they habitually find themselves."[2] Yet, at the same time, no relationship is more fulfilling.

"Marriage then becomes a great adventure, a continuous discovery both of oneself and of one's mate. It becomes a daily broadening of one's horizon, an opportunity of learning something new about life, about human existence, about God. This is why in the beginning of the Bible God says, 'It is not good that man should be alone.' Man here means the human being: 'It is not good that the human being should be alone.' The human being needs fellowship; he needs a partner, a real encounter with others. He needs to understand others, and to sense that others understand him.

"Such is the very intention of God in instituting marriage, according to the Bible. Alone, a man marks time and becomes very set in his ways. In the demanding confrontation which marriage constitutes, he must ever go beyond himself, develop, grow up into maturity. When marriage is reduced to mere symbiosis of two persons essentially hidden from one another, peaceful though such life may sometimes be, it has completely missed its goal. Then it is not solely the marriage which has failed, but both husband and wife. They have failed in their calling as a man and a woman. To fail to understand one's spouse is to fail to understand oneself. It is also a failure to grow and

157

to fulfill one's possibilities."[3] So writes Paul Tournier, the eminent Swiss psychiatrist and Christian thinker.

In addition to the dynamics of the husband-wife relationship, there are also the responsibilities of parenting. To a significant degree, parents are the sculptors of their children's lives. They mold their self-image, shape their understanding of God and establish their values. Such a demanding task could not help but challenge the spiritual maturity and personal resources of the parent. Now add to the dynamics of marriage and parenting the demands of the extended family — parents and siblings — and it is easy to see why the family provides a perfect microcosm of life. If we can be truly Christian in our marriage and family lives, then we can be Christian anywhere!

It would be unfair to end this brief introduction without acknowledging that marriage and the family should also provide the truest love and the deepest joy of which we are capable. Few experiences in life can equal the joy of a three-generation Thanksgiving dinner. Nothing is more beautiful than an elderly couple, deeply in love, celebrating their golden wedding anniversary surrounded by their children, their grandchildren, and their great-grandchildren. Such experiences give us a glimpse of marriage and the family as God intended them to be.

When a marriage, a family, functions as it is supposed to, it is the most blessed experience this side of eternity. And it not only makes us better persons, it also enhances our ability to experience life. Family love enables us to risk, to reach out and become involved with life in ways we would never dare risk alone.

Endnotes

[1]Quoted by Robert A. Raines in a sermon entitled "To See Each Other 'Real' Is Resurrection" in *The Splendor of Easter,* edited by Floyd W. Thatcher (Waco: Word Books, 1972), pp. 23,24.

[2]David R. Mace, *Love and Anger in Marriage* (Grand Rapids: Zondervan Publishing House, 1982), p. 12.

[3]Paul Tournier, *To Understand Each Other*, translated by John S. Gilmour (Richmond: John Knox Press, 1962), pp. 30,31.

Chapter 13

THE DIVINE IDEAL

Several years ago Erich Segal wrote *Love Story*, a tenderly funny and poignant story of two young people who fall in love and marry. It became an instant best-seller, but it cannot compare with the real-life love story of the late John and Harriet McCormack, as related by Peggy Stanton in *The Daniel Dilemma*.

"They were married fifty-two years and never spent a night apart....Dr. Billy Graham referred to their marriage as one of the great love stories of our generation. He said there was a very deep spiritual affinity between them that was far more binding than the psychological or the physical. Roger Brooks, their chauffeur of twenty years, declared, 'They were just like newly-weds.'

"Harriet McCormack was eighty-seven years old when she died, and age had worked a cruel toll on her declining years. It had narrowed her vision, forced her to hide her dark eyes behind glasses. Arthritis, stemming from a leg injury, had slowed her walk to infant steps. Even eating had become a chore, the food had to be soft and in small pieces. Once, at a White House State dinner, John McCormack was observed cutting his wife's meat.

"When Harriet was hospitalized in her eighty-seventh year, John took the hospital room next to hers and kept the door open between them at all times so he could hear her if she called during the night. When she was too warm he bathed her forehead. When she was weak he fed her. When she could no longer eat solid foods, he did not; if she had to endure roast mush, he would endure it with her. In the small hours of the morning her soft moan would come, 'John, John, where are you?' and he would scuffle into his slippers and tug on his bathrobe. 'I'm right here, Harriet, don't worry.' When she slipped into the past, he was not impatient. He went with her. 'I'm so glad I can help her there,' he told John Monohan, 'I can remember her brothers and sisters.'

"He sat there day after day, hour after hour, according to Jo Meegan, and would repeat everything. He would recall all their early life together with great fondness. . . .When people talked about sacrifice, he scoffed at them. What did they mean? He wanted to be with Harriet. He was annoyed when anyone suggested duty. Duty wasn't love."[1]

Now, I believe with all my heart that this is what God had in mind when He said: ". . .'It is not good for the man to be alone. I will make a helper suitable for him'" (Gen. 2:18). Yet how few marriages ever approach this divine ideal. Studies indicate that only about 10 percent of all marriages reach their relational potential; the rest struggle along in mediocrity or end in divorce.

" 'In May 1981 the *Detroit Free Press* reported the results of a marriage poll: 80 percent of all couples in the United States would not marry their same mates if they had the opportunity to marry again.' "[2] When Craig Massey, a Christian family counselor, conducted his own poll involving approximately 750 Christian couples, the results were almost identical.[3]

Tragically, marriage, which was created by God to end the loneliness of human beings, is often the loneliest relationship of all. Couples live in the same house, share the same bed, parent the same children, even make "love." Yet they never really touch each other. For all the things they appear to have in common, they are virtual strangers. There's only one thing worse, and that's when one of the partners is so wrapped up in his or her own life, that he or she doesn't even realize the tragic emptiness of their marriage relationship.

How far short of our bright expectations this tragic reality falls. Almost everyone approaches marriage with high anticipation. Newly-weds may not understand much about marriage, or the commitments they have made, but they do expect to be happy. At a marriage seminar, couples were asked to list their premarital expectations. The men expected sex every night, and the women expected candy, roses and help with the dishes. In short, both husbands and wives expected to "live happily ever after."

In his book on premarital counseling, Aaron Rutledge writes: ". . . modern couples expect marriage to provide self-development and fulfillment; mutual expressions of

163

affection; satisfaction of sexual urges; a sharing of child-rearing responsibilities; a mutual experience of status, belongingness and security; and shared interests in friends, recreation, worship, and creative work.

"In the history of mankind," Rutledge concludes, "never have so many expected so much from marriage and family life."[4]

Reformed pastor Frederick Herwaldt, Jr., echoes Rutledge's conclusions and even goes a step further: "I believe marriage is in trouble today because society and the church have a faulty view of it — a myth of this human, delightful, yet flawed, institution. Though a few lone voices speak against the institution, most laud a romantic image of marriage as life's ultimate source of true joy."[5]

If Herwaldt means that marriage is in trouble because couples expect to miraculously "live happily after," then I agree with him. But if he means that we shouldn't expect to achieve the divine ideal, no matter how hard we work at it, no matter how committed we are, then I must disagree with him. We live in a fallen world and, consequently, we must contend with our sinfulness. But God still intends for marriage to be a special relationship, one in which two people experience the deepest intimacy and the most complete fulfillment of which they are capable. To settle for anything less is to deny the divine ideal.

Such a relationship is not possible, though, unless both the husband and the wife are truly in fellowship with the Lord and in touch with themselves. That is not to say that by focusing on the spiritual life, a couple will automatically have a satisfying marriage. Rather it means that until an individual is intimate with God, and transparent with himself, he really can't develop a deep and fulfilling relationship with anyone else, including his spouse. However, even when a person is deeply spiritual, he must still make a conscious choice to invest the time and energy required to make his marriage all that God intends. And he must consciously work at developing the skills which a meaningful marriage demands.

As a pastor, I have the opportunity to conduct many weddings, and I always encourage couples to receive Holy Communion during the ceremony. Not only is it a deeply spiritual act, but, it also provides a unique opportunity for me to address the special reponsibilities that are involved in marriage.

The Communion elements symbolize the heart and soul of all true relationships. The bread exemplifies true love — the gift of one's self. Taking the bread Jesus said, ". . .'Take and eat; this is my body'" (Matt. 26:26). " 'Greater love has no one than this, that one lay down his life for his friends'" (John 15:13). The cup then portrays the gift of forgiveness. Again Jesus said, "'. . .This is my blood of the covenant, which is poured out. . .for the forgiveness of sins'" (Matt. 26:27,28).

In marriage we must love one another like that — selflessly, to the very laying down of our lives — that is, our interests, our desires, our needs. We do it for our beloved but we also do it for our marriage, for the good of this holy relationship. We give it priority time and energy lest love be lost in the press of living.

I addressed this thought in a note I wrote to Leah, our only daughter, on the eve of her wedding:

"Leah, Marriage is what you make it.
Under God,
it must be the most important single thing,
in all your life.
If your marriage is good, you can overcome anything —
financial adversity,
illness,
rejection,
anything.
If it is not good,
there is not enough success in the world
to fill the awful void.
Remember, nothing, absolutely nothing,
is more important than your marriage,
so work at it with love and thoughtfulness
all the days of your life.

"Guard it against all intruders.
Remember your vows:
You have promised,
before God and your families,
to forsake all others
and cleave only to each other.
Marriage is made of time, so schedule time together.
Spend it wisely in deep sharing.
Tell him, tell her, your whole heart.
Spend it wisely in fun — laugh and play.
Do things together, go places.
Spend it wisely in worship — pray together.
Spend it wisely in touching — hold each other.

"Remember, a song isn't a song until you sing it.
And a bell isn't a bell until you ring it.
And love isn't love until you give it away,

>   so give all of your love to each other,
>   all the days of your life."[6]

About three years ago, as I was flying to a conference in Minnesota, I began reminiscing and ended up writing Brenda a letter, recapping the twenty-five-year history of our courtship and marriage. It was an incredible experience, giving me the opportunity to relive and re-experience the precious moments of our shared past. With Brenda's permission I would like to share portions of that letter.

"Brenda, you really are an extraordinary person, not absolutely perfect, but definitely extraordinary, definitely special.

"You are an unusually beautiful woman. We've been married almost twenty years and I still light up when you walk into a room. I'm so proud to be seen with you. Without a doubt I look better when we're together.

"You are gracious and elegant. Under your touch leftovers become an occasion, and you can turn an ordinary drop-in evening into a festive event. You make cheese and crackers more elegant than caviar. What a joy to bring friends home to our house.

"You are supportive. I cannot remember a single occasion when you made me feel like a failure or a poor provider. Not that you haven't had occasion to.

"Remember the Christmas, nearly twenty years ago, when we had no money and gifts were out of the question? Instead of bemoaning our unhappy plight we decided to be creative. I remember driving to the river bottom and collecting driftwood and dried weeds and wild flowers. You made your folks an arrangement from wild flowers and dried 'weeds.' From a second piece of driftwood, I made mine a TV lamp, which sits in their bedroom still. Somehow, they seem to cherish those homemade gifts, above the more expensive, store-bought ones of later years. Maybe it's because love has a way of turning discarded things into treasures of the heart.

"Do you remember the first time we had guests for dinner at the parsonage in Holly? Right after we said grace, you heard a splashing noise in the kitchen, and discovered a mother mouse and her five babies swimming in the soapy dishwater. Without a complaint you did those six mice in. Thankfully, our guests were 'country folk' and unfazed by it all.

"When the moths invaded us each summer, instead of complaining, you turned a miserable situation into a game. After switching off all the lights, you turned on the gas burners, on the kitchen range, and fried those dive-bombing bugs! At other times we took turns using the vacuum cleaner to catch them. No complaints from you, no tearful depressions, not even envy toward those pastors who were faring better than we. Just an amazing ability to be content in all situations. How fortunate I was. How fortunate I am."

Another time I wrote:

"You've given me so much —
more than I ever imagined possible.
Simple things but rare —
a quiet place away from the noisy world,
a gentle love without demands,
inspiration without expectations.
Common things too, of uncommon value —

a cup of coffee when I come home at night,
        a fire in the fireplace,
        supper on the stove.
        I give you me,
        now and always.
        I am yours
in a way no one else can ever be yours,
        in a way I can never be
        in relationship with anyone else.
I will love you all the days of my life.
When you are lonely I will comfort you.
When you are tired I will refresh you.
When you are sick I will care for you.
I will share all your joys and sorrows
        your whole life long.
We will celebrate growing old together,
        warmed against winter's chill
        by the memories of a lifetime
        cherished and shared."

There's more, but I think you get the picture. That letter and the poem became a door which led to hours of fond memories and intimate sharing. Perhaps you are thinking that's well and good for me but you're not a writer. Don't despair. There are other ways of cherishing the memories of yesterday, other ways of recalling and sharing your mutual past.

History sharing is one, reminiscing. We do a lot of this when we are sitting around the table after we've finished eating, or when we are spending an evening in front of the fireplace. Even now Leah and her husband, Todd, love to hear about our childhood, our favorite holiday, how we met, our first date, or a hundred other things that bring the joys of yesterday back with a nostalgic rush of emotion. These are little things, to be sure, small expressions of our love, but they help us keep romance in our marriage.

Unfortunately, far too few couples take the time to love in this way. If they would do so, not only would they experience a deepening of their marriage, but also a greater appreciation of their shared past and a clearer understanding of the present. How sad that so few couples realize the importance of celebrating "the now." Remember, today's joys will be tomorrow's memories.

If you are really serious about experiencing love in your marriage, then make the most of today. Live it to the fullest. Love completely, totally. The wise man wrote:

". . . rejoice in the wife of your youth.

". . . be captivated by her love."

Proverbs 5:18,19

Endnotes

[1]Peggy Stanton, *The Daniel Dilemma* (Dallas: Word Incorporated, 1978), pp. 41,43,57.

[2]Craig Massey, "Why Don't You Talk To Me?" *Moody*, June 1982, p. 17. This article originally appeared in *MOODY MONTHLY.*

[3]Ibid.

[4]Aaron Rutledge, *Pre-Marital Counseling* (Cambridge, Massachusetts: Schenkman, 1966), p. 25.

[5]Frederick Herwaldt, Jr., "The Ideal Relationship and Other Myths About Marriage," *Christianity Today,* 9 Apr. 1982, p. 30.

[6]Richard Exley, *Notes to Leah,* (unpublished).

Chapter 14

MAKING THE DIVINE
IDEAL REAL

Even as Brenda and I reminisce, even as we cherish the memories of yesterday — our first date, homecoming, our first apartment, Leah's birth — we are careful not to be tempted to try and recapture those by-gone days. That would be counter-productive. We use our past only as a way of enriching the present. And even as we look back, we also look ahead, knowing full well that how we live and relate today will determine, to a significant degree, what our future will be.

We look forward to growing old together. We dream of one day retiring to a modest home in the Rockies where I can write at my leisure. We fantasize about white Christmases, about Todd and Leah coming home with our grandbabies. And because the future is so precious, we dare not let love and romance be lost. We fully expect to be more in love thirty years from now than we are today, but we realize that it won't just happen. To make that dream a reality, we will have to keep romance in our marriage every day of our lives.

For that to become a reality, we will have to add to our love the holy art of forgiveness. Which brings us back to the elements of Holy Communion, the symbols which represent the principles that are at the heart and soul of marriage.

As unbelievable as it may seem to the young couple as they stand in the glow of their love on this, their wedding day, they will sin against their marriage. And when they do (as inevitably they must, such being the nature of our fallen race), then only the cup of forgiveness will be able to restore the divine ideal.

I addressed this issue, as well, in my notes to Leah on the eve of her wedding. From personal experience I wrote:

"Unfortunately, even the best marriages suffer wounds.
We sin against our marriage, against our love.
Sometimes we do it deliberately,
in selfishness or anger,
but usually we sin unintentionally,
thoughtlessly.
What happens next is critical.
It will decide the fate of your marriage.
You must forgive the offending spouse.
It won't be easy.

He or she has hurt you.
Everything within you cries out for vengeance,
tempts you to know
the ugly satisfaction of 'getting even.'
Don't yield to that temptation.
If you do
you will only wound your marriage further.
Forgive him, or her, as the case may be.
If you can't do it
simply because you love your spouse,
do it for your marriage,
for the relationship,
which is more important than either of you."[1]

In short, don't spoil today by dwelling on past failures, your own or your spouse's. If you insist on nursing yesterday's hurts, you will become a prematurely old and bitter person, forfeiting any chance you may have of enjoying the present. We've all been hurt by those we love most. Some of us more than others, I'll grant you that, but the only hope for achieving the divine ideal lies in our ability to forgive and forget. We can't afford to let past hurts rob us of today's joy, nor can we allow them to steal our future happiness.

Forgiveness is not free, as some suppose. In order to forgive us, Jesus had to pay; it cost Him His life. He was willing to suffer and die only because He loved us more than He loved Himself. The same principle applies to forgiveness in marriage. The one who pays must be the offended spouse, the one who has been hurt. He or she, as the case may be, must die to his or her rights.

In *As for Me and My House,* Walter Wangerin, Jr., explains it this way: "Forgiveness is a willing relinquishment of certain rights. The one sinned against chooses not to demand her* rights of redress for the hurt she has suffered. She does not hold her spouse accountable for his sin, nor enforce a punishment upon him, nor exact a payment from him, as in 'reparations.' She does not make his life miserable in order to balance accounts for her own misery, though she might feel perfectly justified in doing so, tit for tat: 'He deserves to be hurt as he hurt me.'

"In this way [please note this carefully] she steps outside the systems of law; she steps into the world of mercy. She makes possible a whole new economy for their relationship: not the cold-blooded and killing machinery of rules, rights, and privileges, but the tender and nourishing care of mercy, which always rejoices in the growth, not the guilt or the pain, of the other. This is sacrifice. To give up one's rights is to sacrifice something of one's self — something hard-fought-for in the world.

". . . forgiveness is giving love when there is no reason to love and no guarantee that love will be returned. The spouse is simply not lovable right now! Forgiveness is repaying evil with kindness, doing all the things that love requires — even when you don't feel the love; for you can do love also in the desert days when you do not feel loving.

"Only when a pure, unexpected, unreasonable, and undeserved gift-giving appears in the marriage does newness enter in and healing begin. This is grace. . . . Finally, gift-giving is the greatest sacrifice of all, for it is the complete 'giving away' of one's self."[2]

---

*Although the author uses the feminine pronoun, this is not meant to imply that the woman is always the innocent party or that the woman is the only one required to practice forgiveness.

It would be easier to forgive, I think, if there were some guarantees, if we could be assured that our spouse would change, that he or she would never sin against us again. But there are no guarantees. Forgiveness, like love, is a risk. Our mercy may be mistaken for weakness. Our spouse may get the wrong idea and feel free to disregard our feelings, free to abuse the marriage covenant.

Realism forces me to acknowledge that there are those who seem immune even to the miracle of forgiveness. Some spouses seem determined to sin, even against the gift of mercy. Still, we must forgive, for if we do not our marriage is doomed. Forgiveness too may fail, but it is the only chance we have of recovering the divine ideal.

When forgiveness is freely given and fully received, a miracle takes place. Anger dies. Hurt and bitterness are replaced with love. Tenderness resides where once hostile silence reigned. Communication is restored. Old hurts are replaced by bright hopes. Once again marriage is a safe place in a demanding world. Your spouse is a safe person, your helper, your lover, your friend and closest confidant.

When love and forgiveness are the daily disciplines of marriage, the daily bread that nourishes the relationship, then the divine ideal can become an ever-increasing reality. You can know the wonder of growing old with the one you've loved and shared your whole life.

You can look forward to the kind of contentment Phyllis Valkins describes in a *Denver Post* article entitled "A Kiss for Kate":

"Every afternoon when I come on duty as the evening nurse, I would walk the halls of the nursing home, pausing at each door to chat and observe. Often, Kate and Chris, their big scrapbooks in their laps, would be reminiscing over the photos. Proudly, Kate showed me pictures of by-gone years: Chris tall, blonde, handsome. Kate pretty, dark-haired, laughing. Two young lovers smiling through the passing seasons. How lovely they looked now, sitting there, the light shining on their white heads, their time-wrinkled faces smiling at remembrance of the years, caught and held forever in the scrapbook."[3]

She concludes: "How little the young know of loving. How foolish to think they have a monopoly on such a precious commodity. The old know what loving truly means; the young can only guess."[4]

This is the divine ideal — the meaning of marriage.

Endnotes

[1]Richard Exley, *Notes to Leah* (unpublished).

[2]Walter Wangerin, Jr., *As for Me and My House* (Nashville: Thomas Nelson, Inc., 1987), pp. 79-81.

[3]Phyllis Valkins, "A Kiss For Kate," *Reader's Digest,* Aug. 1982. (Originally published in *The Denver Post.*)

[4]Ibid.

Chapter 15

THE MEANING OF MARRIAGE — PART 1
"Accepting and Forgiving"

How little most newly-weds know of marriage. They have spent weeks, even months, planning the wedding, but have given almost no thought to marriage itself. And what thinking they have done is of the most unrealistic kind.

One frustrated young husband confessed, "I soon discovered that my wife's idea of a perfect husband was a blend of John Wayne's masculinity, Johnny Carson's wit, and Father Flanagin's sensitivity.

"What chance," he moaned, "do I have of living up to that?"

Of course, he had his own unrealistic expectations, and, when pressed, confessed that his premarital vision of the ideal wife combined the purity of St. Theresa with the youthful beauty of Elizabeth Taylor, plus the culinary genius of Betty Crocker. Needless to day, the realities of married life left both of these naive young idealists in a daze.

You're probably thinking that this illustration is a bit absurd. Granted, that young man was likely overstating the case a bit, but I believe his point is well taken. In my experience as a pastoral counselor, I have discovered that almost nothing creates more anger and frustration in marriage than unrealized expectations. Depending on the personalities involved, these disappointments may produce weeks of sulking silence or vicious verbal bouts. Either way the young marriage is wounded, sometimes fatally.

Still, most couples survive this rude awakening, though few ever really grasp the true meaning of marriage. For them it is hardly more than a social norm. Oh, they pay lip service to its spiritual dimensions, but beyond that they apparently have no idea of what the Creator had in mind when He said:

" ' . . ."For this reason a man will leave his father and mother and be united to his wife, and the two will become one flesh." ' "

Matthew 19:5

The first meaning (purpose) of marriage is companionship. Man/woman was not created to be alone. Although sin had not yet entered the world, and in spite of the fact that Adam lived in perfect fellowship with God, the Lord still concluded that it was not good for him to be alone. (See Gen. 2:18.) Which is just another way of saying that no matter how good our relationship with the Lord may be, we still need the companionship of another human being in order to be fulfilled as persons. Although marriage cannot be expected to meet all of our belonging needs, it does play a unique and vital role. It is the central relationship around which all others must revolve.

As we have already noted, marriage doesn't just "happen." It is more than a ceremony, more than public vows and pastoral prayers. The wedding formalizes a bonding process that has developed through courtship, and it is vitally important, not only for legal reasons, but for spiritual and psychological reasons as well. Still, the real work of marriage begins after the ceremony.

The first work is a transfer of allegiance: "For this reason a man [or woman] will *leave* his father and mother..." (Gen. 2:24).

On the eve of our daughter's wedding, I told her: "After tomorrow you will be Todd's wife. Our daughter still, but not in the same way, not ever again. From that moment forward your first allegiance, your first loyalty, belongs to your husband. Our home will no longer be your home. With Todd you will now make a new home of your own. You must 'leave' before you can 'cleave.'"

This does not mean that the new couple is no longer in relationship with their parents, only that the parent-child relationship has changed. Whereas, before, it was "the" primary relationship, it has now become a secondary one. Still important, to be sure, but not as important. In fact, couples who lack this continuing relationship with their

179

parents find it harder to develop their own oneness. Since they have never had an intimate family relationship, they now find it difficult to trust one another enough to establish their own intimacy. Such trust can, and must be, developed if they are to truly "be married," but for them it will require a greater effort. And since they lack a proper parental model for marriage, they will have to generate one of their own.

Brenda and I were fortunate in this respect. Our parents provided both a positive role model, and a strong, supportive extended family. Developing our own marriage identity was further enhanced by the fact that the ministry took us to a small parish nearly a thousand miles from "home." As a consequence, there was a physical "leaving," as well as an emotional one.

Still, there were obstacles to be overcome. Roles had to be defined — who was going to reconcile the checkbook and pay the bills, who was going to carry out the trash, who got the bathroom first in the morning, and a host of other seemingly trivial details. Nonetheless, it was the successful resolution of these "little" details which set the tone for our marriage.

Then there was the matter of lifestyles. I came from a structured family. My father worked an eight-to-five, five-day-a-week job, and we had three meals a day and on schedule. Brenda, on the other hand, was the product of a more flexible family structure. Her father worked shift work and, as a consequence, the family had irregular mealtimes. They had one meal together each day and when they ate it depended upon Ben Roy's work schedule. The rest of the time they all fared for themselves. You can imagine the conflict this difference in lifestyles created for Brenda and me. I expected three meals a day and at regular intervals. Brenda expected to cook one meal a day at whatever time was most convenient.

Still, one of the biggest adjustments centered on this matter of allegiance. Alone in our home there was no problem, but let us be with Brenda's folks and the dynamics of our family relationships changed, whether we were in their home or our own. This situation continued for several years before we finally identified what was happening. I love Brenda's parents, and it was always a pleasure to be with them, but I often found myself resenting them, especially her mother, Hildegard. Needless to say, these feelings caused no little tension, both internally for me, and externally between Brenda and me. Further complicating matters was the fact that I couldn't put my finger on exactly what it was that was troubling me.

Finally I began to pray about my feelings, and through prayer I was able to identify their source. The problem wasn't Hildegard, it was us, Brenda and me. When we were with the Wallaces, the balance of allegiance shifted ever so subtly. Normally, Brenda was my wife first, Leah's mother second, and then Hildegard's daughter. When we were with her parents, the roles were exactly reversed — she was Hildegard's daughter first. I'm sure something of the same nature happened to me when we were with my parents, but since Brenda doesn't seem to need as much attention as I do, in that situation the impact on our marriage was not as obvious.

Once I finally identified the source of my frustration, we were able to talk about it and come to an understanding. Since we saw our parents so infrequently, it was natural for Brenda to give priority attention to her mother. I needed to realize that fact, accept it, and stop resenting it. Brenda, on the other hand, determined to make a special effort to nurture our relationship, even when we were with her parents. It wasn't that I required more of her time, just an awareness on her part that even "now," even "here," her first allegiance belonged to our marital family rather than to her parental family.

I share this incident simply as a way of illustrating the absolute necessity for married couples to make their marriage, and their spouse, their first and highest allegiance under God. The resulting oneness is called *bonding*.

In his book, *Intimate Behavior,* Dr. Desmond Morris writes: "Bonding refers to the emotional covenant that links a man and woman together for life. It is the specialness which sets those two lovers apart from every other person on the face of the earth."[1] This bonding is what the scriptures are referring to when they say of the married couple, ". . .and they will become one flesh" (Gen. 2:24).

In marriage each of us is uniquely related to our spouse. I am Brenda's *only* husband, and she is my *only* wife. In all the other relationships of our lives we are one among many. One child among several children in our families, one friend among many friends, one student among many students, one of many players on a team, one of several employees on the job, one of many. . . . Not now, not here! For the first time ever I am the *only* one to her, and she is the only *one* to me.

This blessed oneness is embryonic to begin with. That is, it is true in the spirit of our relationship, but not in the reality of our day to day lives. Two separate and distinct individuals are not suddenly one simply because the minister pronounces them husband and wife. They *become* one flesh. It takes time and commitment, not to mention love and hard work.

Because she loves him completely, he can trust her with his life. He tells her his hidden fears, the secret doubts he has never dared share with anyone. In her presence, in the circle of her love, nothing he thinks or says seems foolish or insignificant. And as he tells her his whole heart — not all at once, but over an extended period — they become one. She takes his life into her own. His joy is now hers. His childhood and adolescence are now part of her past too. His pain is hers as well; and his victories, his achievements, become theirs, the "stuff" of which their oneness is made. This, too, is the meaning of marriage.

Because he loves her completely, selflessly, she can trust him with her heart. In the quiet of evening, after the children have been put to bed, she tells him the story of her life. Not just the past with its memories, both good and bad, but the events of her day as well. The phone call she received from an old friend, the gist of the conversation she shared with a neighbor over coffee, something one of the children did. Little things, insignificant taken alone, but together they are the fabric of her life. And in the sharing they become part of his life as well. They become their life, their oneness.

I am speaking of the "divine ideal," of course, and the reality of marriage is often something altogether different. Yet, if we don't speak of the ideal, then we have no worthy model, no goal to strive for, no true measurement for our marital relationships. Still, when our marriage doesn't measure up, the ideal can become a continuing source of frustration and pain. How we deal with this pain will determine the climate of our marriage and the shape of our future.

Some couples make peace with their pain; they give up their dreams and live out their lives in mediocrity. They are together, but not intimate. Silence has become a way of life for them.

Others live in a kind of "cold war." They tolerate each other, but barely, never missing an opportunity to let their dissatisfaction be known. Divorce is out of the question, but so is love. He has mastered the unholy art of saying, "Yes, Dear," in a way which clearly says she is not dear, at least not dear to him! For her part, she has perfected a contemptuous glance, accompanied by a certain pursing of her lips, that can stop him dead in his tracks, even across a room full of people.

Then there are those couples who quarrel bitterly. Their marriage is a war zone; verbal and emotional abuse are the order of the day. Angry words leave their fragile self-images sorely wounded. And, finally, there are the martyrs, those sad souls who suffer in silence, those who have made a lifelong pact with self-pity. The one thing all these couples have in common is loneliness — and misery.

Surely there must be a better way. Some way of transcending their differences, some way of releasing their hurts and anger, some way of communicating their love, some way of starting over. There is, but it won't be easy. And everything within will fight against it.

If your marriage has failed to live up to this divine ideal, you will most likely be tempted to blame your spouse. Instead, you must accept your share of the responsibility and determine that you will change. You will be tempted to excuse yourself, to justify your shortcomings as simply being "just the way you are." That may appear to be true to you, or it may simply seem like the easiest way out, but it is not true — at least not totally. The real reason we do things the way we do, the reason we refuse to change, is not because that is "just the way we are" so much as it is the result of our ingrained selfishness.

Selfishness, as we all know, is the original sin. Adam and Eve insisted on doing things their way rather than God's. This same self-centered spirit is at work in all of us, undermining not only our marriages, but all the relationships of our lives. And this is both our condemnation and our salvation. Our condemnation, because sin always steals and destroys. Our salvation, because sin can be forgiven, and the sinner can be changed!

If we claim that our behavior is fated, or if we explain it as an immutable quality of our personality, that it's "just the way we are," then our situation is hopeless. Personalities, as any counselor knows, are almost impossible to change. On the other hand, to admit that our marital failures are rooted in sin invites the power of God into our situation. And God can eradicate the sin and transform the sinner.

Once we have owned our "sin," we must make a commitment to live selflessly rather than selfishly. Now we choose to spend Sunday afternoon with our wife, rather than ensconced in front of the TV watching NFL football. Now we determine to develop an interest in the things that concern our spouse, rather than complaining that our wife or our husband never talks to us. Now we take the initiative for being the kind of husband, the kind of wife, that God intends us to be. And, as a result, the climate of our marriage begins to change.

Yet, it would be naive to pretend that all the responsibility for the emptiness in any marriage belongs to one partner. In truth, both spouses have a share, even in those situations where one is blatantly in the wrong. Therefore, it is now time to address the "sins" of our spouse. We cannot avoid this unpleasant task. We cannot simply pretend that he/she has not sinned against us. Such pretending simply becomes another obstacle to intimacy. Unacknowledged sin is like a misplaced piece of furniture in the soul of our marriage. Until it is forgiven, removed, we will continually bump into it. Certain topics will invariably be "off limits"; there will always be an unspoken accusation, a lingering shadow of guilt.

Our purpose is not to accuse our mate, nor to somehow shift the blame from ourselves. In fact, the only reason we can bring ourselves to face this unpleasant task is so we might forgive our spouse. It is the one thing which remains to be done before we can hope to experience the blessed oneness that our hearts so hunger for. We must take the cup of forgiveness and extend it to our spouse.

But forgiveness is not easy. Justice demands that we get our "pound of flesh." Our feelings scream for revenge, someone has to pay. Why should we be the only one to suffer? Why should the perpetrator, our spouse, get off scot-free? Yet experience has taught us that revenge is never worth the cost — it will bankrupt our marriage. When we refuse to forgive, when we choose to hold onto our hurts, and our anger, we are choosing them over our spouse, over our marriage.

True forgiveness, however, is impossible until we have "processed" our feelings. Hurt and anger do not simply go away just because we decide to forgive our spouse. In fact, if we forgive without dealing with our feelings, it will be an empty act, hardly worth the effort.

In my work with hurting couples I frequently recommend that the wounded spouse write a letter to the offender in which he/she details the spouse's sins and describes how those sinful acts have made him/her feel. This is usually a lengthy and often exhausting experience, for as the person reviews the offenses he or she seems to relive them as well, re-experiencing the actual emotions all over again. Rather than sharing the letter with his/her spouse, I ask the offended party to bring it in and share it with me. After we have fully explored the issues and exhausted his/her emotional residue, I then ask him/her to specifically forgive the offending spouse. His/her forgiveness must be specific, not general, because he/she has been sinned against specifically not generally.

Next I help the offended spouse prepare a detailed and accurate list of the marital transgressions. When this list is completed, he/she is now ready to confront his/her mate, not in anger, but in love. The purpose of this meeting is to acquaint the husband/wife with the specific sins he/she has committed against the marriage, and the hurt it has inflicted. It does little good to be forgiving if the offending party does not know that he/she is being forgiven, and for what.

Since the wounded partner has already dealt with his/her emotions, and has already pronounced forgiveness, he/she can approach this face-to-face meeting free from the volatile emotions which would otherwise likely sabotage it. Since he/she understands clearly the purpose of the meeting, he/she can move directly to forgiveness and a declaration of his/her love. Having executed the mechanics of forgive-

187

ness, he/she is now free to get on with the task of living out that forgiveness.

Endnotes

[1]Desmond Morris, *Intimate Behavior* (New York: Random House, 1971), p. 73.

Chapter 16

THE MEANING OF MARRIAGE — PART 2
"Becoming One Flesh"

While unforgiveness is the primary cause of marital dysfunction, there is a second and equally widespread cause — ignorance. Since we've already dealt with the big one — unforgiveness — it is now time to address the second.

Very few people enter marriage with any real idea of how to have a deeply fulfilling relationship. Beyond a few tips they may have picked up from observing other, less than ideal, marriages, they don't have a clue as to what it takes to make a marriage successful. Somehow they believe it will just naturally "all work out." Unfortunately, this is seldom the case.

When Brenda and I married, we were as ignorant as could be, but we did have good role models in our parents. Still, beyond a firm conviction that marriage was for life, we had little or no idea how it worked. Needless to say, we had our share of arguments. In fact, we had been married less than a week when our happy home went up in smoke. Inadvertently, I had left my underwear on the bathroom floor after I finished bathing. When Brenda walked into the bathroom a little later, she discovered them and asked me to put them in the dirty clothes hamper.

To this day I'm not sure why I responded the way I did. Picking up my underwear was really no big thing. I wasn't in the habit of leaving my things lying around, and I certainly didn't expect Brenda to pick up after me. Still, I thought she might this once, so I called from the living room: "Why don't you do it for me? You're already in there."

At that moment Brenda undoubtedly had a vision in which she saw herself picking up after me for the next 50 years, and not just my underwear either, but my dirty socks and shirts as well. That wasn't her idea of an ideal marriage, and she wasn't about to set a bad precedent. I can understand that now, but when she kindly insisted that I come and put my clothes in the hamper, I felt she was challenging my position as the head of the home.

With determination, I marched into the bedroom where Brenda was now standing and reminded her that less than a week earlier she had vowed a solemn vow, in the presence of our friends, our families, and before God. I said: "Not only did you promise to forsake all others and cleave only to me. Not only did you pledge your love and faithfulness in sickness and in health, for better or for worse, for richer or for poorer. Not only did you promise, before God, to love and honor me, but you also vowed to obey me." Then I delivered the coup de grace: "If you meant your wedding vows, you will pick up my underwear."

Well, I can tell you, that was the wrong approach. Not only did Brenda refuse to pick up the now "infamous" underwear but she retreated into an impenetrable silence. After several hours in which not a single word was spoken, I finally gave in. First I put my dirty clothes in the hamper, and then I apologized. This was just the first of many domestic quarrels which threatened the happiness of our young marriage. Looking back now, almost 23 years later, we can laugh at our childishness, but at the time it was deadly serious.

And that's not the half of it. Later there were other, more significant quarrels. In fact, there were times when we were so unhappy that we might have considered a divorce had that option been available to us. It wasn't. To our way of thinking, Christians did not divorce. I heartily concur with Walter Wangerin, Jr., who testified concerning his own marital disappointments: "And the thing that neither of us would even contemplate was divorce. We were stuck with each other. Let the world call that imprisonment; but I say it gave us the time, and God the opportunity, to make a better thing between us. If we could have escaped, we would have. Because we couldn't we were forced to choose the harder, better road."[1]

For us "the harder, better road" included not only forgiveness, but a genuine commitment to our marriage.

We each determined to give it priority time and energy. And about eight years into our marriage, I began to discover some marriage tools, quite unexpectedly.

As a pastor, I found myself ministering to troubled couples with increasing frequency. The situations they shared with me were not much different from my own struggles. Unfortunately, I had no better answers for them than I had for myself. In desperation, I began reading everything I could get my hands on concerning Christian marriage and family life. In addition, I attended several marriage seminars and workshops. My expressed purpose was to improve my skills as a pastor, but a far greater benefit was the insights I was getting about myself and our marriage. Brenda and I spent long hours discussing these "discoveries" and how we could implement them in our relationship.

I don't want to leave you with the wrong impression, so let me hasten to add that I don't think we ever had a "bad" marriage, just a mediocre one. We never argued in public, never took separate vacations, or abused one another. We simply weren't intimate in the biblical sense; we weren't "one flesh." We always loved each other, but sometimes we couldn't seem to make contact. Old hurts inhibited our communication. Misunderstandings undermined our closeness. And we were lonely in our marriage. In frustration I had sought emotional fulfillment in my work, which had only increased the emptiness between us.

With the new insights we were gaining about the dynamics of marriage, those things begin to change. Not instantly, not without a concentrated effort on our part, but they were changing just the same. In fact, our marriage improved in direct proportion to the marriage skills we were acquiring, and the amount of ourselves that we were willing to invest in the relationship. Today, almost 15 years later, I can truly say that our marriage is the crowning achievement of our lives. It's not perfect, and we still have to work at it on a daily basis, but it is the most blessed relationship I could ever imagine.

On a more specific note, let me share some guidelines that have served Brenda and me well these past 22 years. We call them the "Ten Commandments for a Healthy Marriage":

1. Protect your day off at all costs and spend it together as a couple, and as a family.

If an emergency makes it impossible for us to have our regularly scheduled time together, we reschedule another day immediately. Nothing is more important than the time we share!

2. Eat dinner together.

Even when we have a simple meal, Brenda makes it an occasion by lighting candles and turning off the T.V. Dinner conversation is a time for sharing and making memories. Issues can be dealt with at another time.

3. Go to bed together.

Nothing undermines intimacy faster than separate bedtimes. This too is a time for sharing and for touching. It's an opportunity to touch base with each other, to make sure we haven't let our hectic schedules cause us to drift apart. Without these "set times" for togetherness we might lose contact with each other in the "busyness" of life.

4. Don't hold a grudge.

If you insist on nursing yesterday's hurts, you will become a prematurely old and bitter person, forfeiting any chance you may have of enjoying the present. We've all been hurt by those we love most. Some of us more than others, I'll grant you that, but the only hope for our marriage lies in our ability to forgive and forget. Don't let past hurts rob you of today's joy!

5. Don't take separate vacations.

Shared experiences bond us together while unshared experiences distance us from one another. Time is one of the most valuable commodities in marriage, so don't spend it foolishly.

6. Never let anything rob your marriage of the sexual joy God intended.

Sex is a gift from God to be enjoyed within the holy bonds of marriage. It is designed as a means of expressing love and giving pleasure, as well as for procreation. While true intimacy is certainly more than sex, it is never less than that.

7. Pray together.

Nothing is more intimate than a person's relationship with God. When you invite your spouse to share that experience with you, you are opening the deepest part of your being to him or her. It is often threatening at first, but the rewards more than justify the effort.

8. Play together.

K.C. Kole, reporting in *Psychology Today*, writes: "All happy couples aren't alike, so there is no single litmus test for a good marriage. But if one studies couples systematically over time, it becomes apparent that many of them share a characteristic that signals, more often that not, a healthy union.

"It's nothing so obvious as a satisfying sexual relationship, or shared interests, or the habit of talking out disputes freely. It is, rather, a capacity for playfulness of a kind that transcends fun and reflects considerably more than the partners' ability to amuse each other. Private nicknames, shared jokes and fantasies, mock insults, make-believe fighting — all these might seem like mere silliness. In fact, they may stand in for, or lubricate, more complex transactions, essential but potentially painful or even destructive."[2]

9. Little things mean a lot.

In fact, they can make the difference between a mediocre marriage and a really good one. It's usually not the expensive gifts or the foreign vacations that determine the quality of a marital relationship, but the little things. A love note in his lunch box or an "unbirthday" card for her. A kind word, help with the children, a listening ear, the feeling that he/she really cares.

10. Pledge yourselves, not only to physical faithfulness, but to emotional fidelity as well.

Brenda and I are determined that our emotional needs will be fulfilled only in our marriage. We do not allow friends, family or career to supply these "belonging needs."

This we provide for each other, and it is the strength of our relationship!

Dorothy Samuel writes: "To know another's body and movements so intimately that each moves in harmony with the other as a waltz partner — this is marriage. To lie down together at the end of a day, to stretch however briefly against the loved one while the physical tensions flee before the soft glory of flesh pressed against flesh; to lie in the dark and share the usually unspoken thoughts, the apologies and compliments each has repressed, the secret dreams and the precious visions — this is marriage. To cap these with a prayer, a shared moment of togetherness in the great ecology of the universe, is to build self into self inextricably as the roots of two sturdy trees mesh the ground of their being. For such, sleep itself becomes a form of intercourse."[3]

This is the ultimate achievement of marriage — this blessed oneness; the merging of self into self until there can never be a Richard without a Brenda, until there can never be a Brenda without a Richard. Yet in our oneness we have lost nothing of our individual personalities. In fact, because of the security of our oneness, each of us is more our individual self than we have ever been. Freed from the fear of misunderstanding or rejection, we can each truly be the self we were meant to be.

The writer of the book of Genesis expresses it poetically: "The man and his wife were both naked, and they felt no shame" (Gen. 2:25). They were one; they had no secrets to hide from each other. They were fully known, each to the other, and they were not ashamed. They had a transparent relationship built on love and trust.

Sexually they were naked and not ashamed. Because they knew each other, in a way that only a husband and wife can know one another, they were joyously uninhibited in their sexuality. They were made for each other, that's what God said, so they took joy in their physical love. It was a gift from God, to be received with thanksgiving and celebrated without shame. It was intended to express love, cultivate intimacy, and provide pleasure, in addition to propagating the race.

Because they were one, because they were truly bonded emotionally, they could give themselves to each other sexually without reservation. And because of their joyous and uninhibited physical union, their emotional intimacy was deepened even further. Without their blessed oneness, the physical act of making love would have been just that — a physical act — empty and unfulfilling. The merging of their flesh without the touching of their souls. That's loneliness of the most haunting kind. Yet, without the expression of their physical love, within the holy bonds of marriage, their emotional and spiritual intimacy would have been incomplete.

Marriage, as God meant it to be, brings it all together — the bread of love to nourish the spirit, the cup of forgiveness to wash our wounds and forgive our failures, to restore our blessed oneness. Nakedness, that nothing need be hidden; transparency, that we may at last know our own self because finally we are known; and physical love, that our aloneness might be swallowed up in the body of our beloved, that our love might give birth to a family!

This is the divine ideal — the meaning of marriage!

Endnotes

[1]Walter Wangerin, Jr., *As For Me and My House* (Nashville: Thomas Nelson, 1987), p. 79.

[2]K.C. Kole, "Playing Together: From Couples That Play," *Psychology Today,* Feb. 1982.

[3]Dorothy T. Samuel, *Fun and Games in Marriage* (Waco: Word Books, 1973), p. 40.

Chapter 17

REMEMBERING OUR ROOTS

No one can be emotionally healthy or spiritually whole without a network of caring people. Dr. E. M. Pattison calls it our "psychological kinship system." According to Dr. Pattison, humans get sick and tend to die if they are out of significant contact with other people. He suggests four kinship groups:

1.   Family: first-degree people such as parents, children or spouse.

2.   Relatives: uncles, aunts, grandparents, and cousins.

3.   Friends: your lifelong collection — but only those active today in your life experience.

4.   Associates: acquaintances from work, church and recreation.[1]

We will address all of these groups before the end of this book, but for now let's turn our attention to the family — those first-degree people who have such a profound influence on our lives. Not just when we're children either, but our whole life long. In my work as a minister, I frequently encounter highly successful people who are unfulfilled and terribly insecure. Almost without exception they had an unhappy childhood.

Dr. Cecil Osborne, the director of Burlingame Counseling Center and author of several books including *The Art of Becoming a Whole Person,* says: "A fundamental psychological law holds that we tend to get our basic self-image from our parents. If they approve of us and give us the warm love and affirmation we need, we come to think of ourselves as okay persons. If we miss out on the three A's — Acceptance, Approval and Affection — we feel that we are not acceptable. This becomes a deep inner conviction, and no amount of success or affirmation in later life can totally eradicate the feeling, 'I don't measure up. I'm not good enough. I'm unacceptable.' "[2]

Without question the family plays a vital role in the development of the individual and in the stability of society as well. Within the family network we define our self-image; not just how we see ourselves, but how we fit into the whole scheme of things. From the family we get our identity, our sense of personal value, our attitude toward life, our values and our sense of belonging.

If our parents were relational people, we will likely grow up to be people persons, warm and caring. If we were part of a family in which the children were loved and treated equally, then chances are we bonded with our siblings, thus establishing a support system for life. And this sense of belonging, of never being totally alone, is often at the very root of a person's self-confidence, his willingness to reach out and take risks.

The longer I live, the more I realize just how fortunate I was. In addition to a very positive relationship with both my parents, and my brothers and sister, I was blessed with an extended family of loving grandparents, aunts and uncles. Although I was never given any reason to think myself better than anyone else, I never doubted my worth as a person either. Within the extended family circle I knew I had a place. I was loved. I was somebody.

My childhood is a patchwork of special memories. When I was five, my Aunt Elsie brought me a quart of home-canned strawberries following my tonsillectomy. By the time I was ten, my Uncle Denny, who owned a water well drilling company, was taking me to work with him. He wasn't much given to talk, but I knew he loved me. After repairing a windmill, we would often stop to shoot prairie dogs with the twenty-two, or hunt pheasants, if they were in season.

With his help I learned to drive before I was 12. Not on the road, of course, but in the pasture. The big power wagon had a stiff clutch, and I could barely see over the steering wheel; still, I've never felt more grown up than I did sitting in the driver's seat of that huge rig bumping across an open field. I do have to tell you though, that Uncle Denny gave me "heck" every time I killed the engine trying to get moving. Nevertheless, I knew I had a special place in his heart.

Then there was my Uncle Ernie, the country pastor, who served small rural churches his whole life. He believed in me and gave me my start in the ministry when I was still a boy in high school. And Aunt Eleanor, who was the most incredible cook in the whole world. Holidays at her house were unbelievable. She was loving and generous, a saint in this small boy's admiring eyes. I can still taste the rich flavor of bedtime snacks at her kitchen table — thick slices of homemade bread covered with homecanned strawberry preserves and thick country cream. A feast fit for a king!

There were my cousins too. James, who in 1958 took me for a late-night ride in his Mercury, when he was home on furlough from the Navy. Darrel who to a 12-year-old boy seemed so exciting in his Air Force uniform. Donna and Esther, who teased me unmercifully, and their "little" brother Orville, whom I teased even more unmercifully. . . .

I loved them, every one, with a little boy's blind love. I love them still today, though the years and this wide country have turned us into virtual strangers. Thinking about it now, as I write these words, tears come to my eyes and a soft sob catches in my throat.

Why do I cry? Because remembering my childhood has touched something deep within me, a sense of loss, I suppose. I weep because we can't ever go back. And I would give almost anything to be 12 again, and spend one more Saturday afternoon with my Uncle Denny. I'd give just about anything to have one more bedtime snack at Aunt Eleanor's kitchen table; one more ride in Cousin James' souped-up Mercury; one more long talk with my Cousin Esther. . . .

Then there was my Grandma Miller — the central figure in my young world. She stood 4'11″ with tightly-curled red hair. As a child I never realized she colored it, but she must have, because it remained the same tint until the day she died. Her entire life was lived on the ragged edge of poverty, but she was rich in spirit.

As I think about her now, she seems like something out of the *Reader's Digest's* most unforgettable character. She was born in 1885 in a small village in Iowa, to a poor but hard-working family. Her parents had little use for what they called "book learnin'." As a consequence, she never learned to read or write, and could barely scribble her own name. As a child I remember watching her struggle to sign her old-age pension check with an indelible pencil.

At the age of 13, still just a wisp of a girl, not quite five feet tall, she married James Lewis Miller. Ten years her senior, he was a big, strapping man, standing three inches over six feet and weighing nearly 260 pounds, with hands the size of hams. The early years of their life together were spent following the railroad across Kansas before finally settling in Greely, Colorado. In about 1910 they homesteaded in the sand hills, near Merino, in the northeastern part of the state.

Grandpa died when I was maybe ten, and I began spending four or five nights a week with Grandma. She never really trusted electricity, so we seldom used it. After dark we lit the kerosine lamps and talked for hours. I can't remember much of what we talked about, no special words of wisdom or insight, but I do remember feeling loved. Grandma Miller made me feel like. . .well, like I could do anything. As I recall those experiences now, I realize that Grandma accepted me as her peer while allowing me to be a child when I needed to. Because of her, I had the best of both worlds — adult company and acceptance, plus the freedom of childhood.

She introduced me to coffee before I started school. It was diluted with thick country cream, but it was still coffee. We poured it from our cups into saucers and drank it the way the Dutch do. Sitting at the breakfast table, sipping coffee with Grandma, I felt like a grownup long before I had any right to. And to this day, a steaming cup of cream-colored coffee can take me back to Grandma's table and the warmth we shared.

There were those who considered her a bit eccentric in her later years. In truth, she was just a throwback to an earlier age. I remember the time I asked her why she carried a loaded pistol in her purse. Without batting an eye she said, "Because if I ever get mad enough to kill someone, I don't want to change my mind while I hunt around for something to do it with!"

Looking back now, these many years later, I think her bark was worse than her bite. I mean, I never knew her to harm anyone, and she was generous to a fault. Still, she did carry that pistol in her purse.

I was always welcome in her world — a world of braided rag rugs, coal oil stoves, and friends from "the old country." Grandma was Dutch, but she lived in a neighborhood of Russian immigrants; consequently, I was exposed to a culture different from my own and to people who spoke with a strange accent (that is, when they didn't lapse into their mother tongue). Grandma loved those old people, and so did I. I could sit by her side for most of an afternoon listening as they talked of people and places I knew nothing about.

I gave up many childhood activities with my friends in order to be with her, and looking back, I can say without a doubt that it was worth it. Only Grandma knows what personal interests and projects she let go unpursued so she could give me her undivided time and attention. She guided me, she modeled her values for me, but she never tried to change me. In her presence I was never afraid of being judged or rejected. Her unconditional love gave me the security to share my real self.

Grandma Miller has been dead for nearly 25 years now, but she lives on in my memory, and her influence shapes me still. She taught me the value of relationships. Under her gentle guidance I learned to experience my deepest feelings and to share them with those I love. She was tenacious, and from her example I learned to "hang tough" and finish what I started. She believed in me and taught me to believe in myself. I am who I am today, at least in part, because of the investment she made in me.

I wish there were some way I could pay her back for all the love she poured into me. As a boy I simply accepted it, never realizing how rare it really was, never thinking to give her thanks. Now it's too late. The best I can do is to try to live in a way which honors her memory. And I can pass her love on. When I become a grandfather, I can try to be the same kind of special friend to my grandchildren. It's the best I can do. I hope it's enough. Knowing her, I'll bet it's exactly what she had in mind.

The final and most important people in my family circle are my parents, a brother named Don, a second brother Bob, and my beautiful little sister. Her name is Sherry, but when she was just a blonde toddler I nicknamed her Toots. We were a family in the truest sense — all for one, one for all. Mom and Dad loved us equally, but not the same, because being unique individuals we each needed our own special kind of love. As a consequence, there was little or no sibling rivalry in our family.

The importance of family is often best seen in the dark hours, when an accident or illness strikes a family member, making death an unwelcome but ever-present threat. In 1985 when our seemingly indestructible father underwent open-heart surgery, the strength of our lifelong bonds stood us in good stead. During the difficult days that followed, including a second emergency operation, we took turns being strong. We strengthened one another. We prayed together when praying alone was more than we could manage. In our combined faith we found the strength to trust God, to place our beloved earthly father into the capable hands of our loving heavenly Father. And as he improved, we filled Dad's hospital room with the healing gift of laughter, as we recalled childhood pranks and family fun.

I've been gone from home for nearly 23 years now, yet I remember it with a special warmth. Childhood memories return like slides projected on a screen. I see my mother, standing in knee-deep snow, silhouetted against the blue sky by winter's dazzling sun, as she hangs wet laundry upon a frozen clothes line. Dad's voice, raised in quiet prayer, drifts in from the living room to wake me in the pre-dawn darkness. Through a bedroom door, left open just a crack, I glimpse Mom on her knees with the Bible open on the bed before her.

Abruptly the scene changes, and I return to a fall night in my childhood. The acetylene hisses to life and the blowtorch stabs the darkness with a bright blue flame.

Adjusting his goggle, Dad bends to his task. A shower of sparks dance in the darkness like a stampede of fire flies. Beneath his torch the discarded machinery slowly becomes scrap iron, which will be sold and the money used to help remodel the church building.

As I grow older, the scene changes again. We've moved from the small Colorado town of my birth to the sprawling suburbs of Houston. It's Saturday morning and the whole family travels across town to watch me play eighth-grade football. Later we have 19-cent MacDonald's hamburgers and fun in the park. Now it's a Saturday afternoon in August and we are on a deserted stretch of beach east of Galveston. We exhaust ourselves playing in the sand and the sea while Mother watches from a distance before spreading out the picnic lunch beneath the canopy of the open sky. It's late when we finally get home. We are contented, but tired; still, no one wonders whether we will go to church in the morning. That's a "given."

Yet a family, like a marriage, doesn't just "happen"; it doesn't evolve simply because a man and woman go through a wedding ceremony and bear children. It takes time, and love, and commitment. In my childhood home both Dad and Mom were the creators of family. Dad was clearly the head of the house. Without being dictatorial or overbearing, he provided the spiritual leadership which gave our family its sense of direction. Mom set the emotional tone. With a special grace she managed to create a house of love, a home in which we were nurtured, both emotionally and spiritually.

Unlike some men who feel that their work ends when they leave the office, Dad helped Mom with both the house and the children. He never made a distinction between "men's work" and "women's work." After supper he helped clear the table and frequently dried the dishes. As a result, today he has three sons who feel that helping their wives is an act of love. All of us are equally adept with the vacuum cleaner or the dishwasher, not to mention scouring powder. And we've each been very much involved in the rearing of our children. Thanks, Dad, for pointing us in the right direction without ever saying a word.

Endnotes

[1]Donald M. Joy, Ph.D., *Bonding: Relationships in the Image of God* (Dallas: Word Incorporated, 1985), pp. 3,4.

[2]Cecil G. Osborne, *The Art of Becoming a Whole Person* (Dallas: Word Incorporated, 1978), pp. 98,99.

Chapter 18

THE MAKING OF A FAMILY

The family is not a cultural phenomenon to be discarded with the changing times. It was conceived in the mind of God. It is the loving gift of a wise and generous Creator. Knowing the unique needs of the man created in His own image, God said: ". . .'It is not good for the man to be alone. I will make a helper suitable for him'" (Gen. 2:18).

". . .So the LORD God caused the man to fall into a deep sleep; and while he was sleeping, he took one of the man's ribs and closed up the place with flesh. Then the LORD God made a woman from the rib he had taken out of the man, and he brought her to the man."

Genesis 2:21,22

Now the man is no longer alone. He has a companion, someone to love and someone to love him, and a helper.

Think of that — God made them helpers, one for the other. And He blessed that union and called it "family." Therefore, we must conclude that God intended for the family to be a helping place. And when it functions as God intended, that's what it is. It provides a loving community in which a child is "helped" to develop his gifts and potentials. It is a safe place in which a child is "helped" to develop the people skills so necessary to live meaningfully in our complex society. And it is a sanctuary in which he is "helped" to learn spiritual values and develop a personal relationship with the living God.

Obviously the most important thing in creating a family is time — time to be together, time to love one another, time to share life's experiences, both great and small. Unfortunately, time seems to be the thing we find hardest to give.

In *What Wives Wish Their Husbands Knew About Women,* Dr. Dobson quotes from an article by Dr. Branfenbrenner, in which he decries the plague of parental absence: "The demands of a job that claim meal times, evenings and weekends as well as day; the trips and moves necessary to get ahead or simply to hold one's own; the increasing time spent communicating, entertaining, going out, meeting social and community obligations, all these produce a situation in which a child often spends more time with a passive babysitter than with a participating parent."[1]

Dr. Dobson then proceeds to substantiate Branfenbrenner's observations: "A team of researchers wanted to learn how much time middle-class fathers spend playing and interacting with their small children. First, they asked a group of fathers to estimate the time spent with their one-year-old youngsters each day, and received an average reply of fifteen to twenty minutes. To verify these claims, the investigators attached microphones to the shirts of small children for the purpose of recording actual parental verbalization. The results are shocking: *The average amount of time spent by these middle-class fathers with their small children was thirty-seven seconds per day! Their direct interaction was limited to 2.7 encounters daily lasting ten to fifteen seconds each.*"[2] (emphasis mine)

It goes almost without saying that the children of such fathers will grow up lacking the sense of family which is absolutely vital to a healthy self-image. Depending upon their motivation, their skills, and their intellect, they may go on to become outstanding successes in their chosen fields. But without a special healing they will not be fulfilled; they will not escape the nagging questions they have about their value as persons. Still, the greatest tragedy may be the fact that they will "sin" against their children in the same way their parents "sinned" against them, thus perpetuating this tragedy from generation to generation. And the likelihood of this happening increases, almost daily, as our world becomes more and more impersonal.

In order to break this deadly cycle, the person driven by self-doubts must find emotional healing in the presence of God, and through the dynamic fellowship of committed believers. He must find a surrogate family, a place to belong. As unlikely as this may sound to the person who has been "alone" all his life, it is possible. In fact, it is happening with increasing frequency. As the Church learns more and more about the relationship between community and personal wholeness, it is providing greater ministry in this area. Over and over again, through the years, I have witnessed God's healing love manifested through small groups of loving believers. The miracles are seldom instantaneous, but they are, nonetheless, dramatic. Take the case of Sterling, for instance:

"I first met him when he came to my office for pastoral counseling. He was only a few days removed from the county jail and newly converted. . . .

"He never knew his father, and his mother abandoned him when he was just a small boy. A kindly aunt took him in and reared him as her own. Still, her love could not heal the wound his parents' rejection had inflicted. By the time he was fourteen, he was a confirmed alcoholic and constantly in trouble with the authorities.

"His incorrigible behavior finally resulted in his being sent to reform school. Unfortunately, that intensified his anger and bitterness, and upon his release he immediately returned to his antisocial behavior. Soon he was serving a sentence in the state penitentiary, then another.

"When he came to see me, he was out on bail awaiting trial for allegedly raping his sixteen-year-old stepdaughter. While in the county jail, he had started reading the Bible and was born again. Now he wanted to know if he could become part of our church. I assured him that he could, and soon he was deeply involved in the life of our fellowship including a growth group which I led once a week. I can still remember the night he told us that he finally felt loved, for the first time in his life, by God and by the group."[3]

At last he was free from his parents' rejection and the debilitating wounds it had left. Now he could get on with the business of becoming a loving husband and father in his own right. It wouldn't be easy, because he had a lifetime of negative behavior to "unlearn," but he knew that with God's help and the support of the group it was possible.

I share Sterling's story, extreme though it is, to make a point. If God could do that for him, then surely He can heal the fears and insecurities that haunt you. There is hope for your family!

And, even if you grew up in a family rich with love and acceptance, you will still need God's help to be the kind of parent your children need. Given the pressures we all face, only a determined decision, backed up by divine help, will enable us to give our families the spiritual and emotional support they must have. As I look back over the past 22 years of marriage, I can testify to God's sufficiency and His faithfulness.

Until Leah entered the fifth grade, her mother and I were serving pastorates in small churches in remote rural areas. Financially, it was a hardship, but what we lacked in money was more than made up for in family time. My office was in the house, so I was always near Leah. Some of my best memories are of her interrupting my sermon preparation for a little tender loving care. Until she was in the sixth grade I was able to drive her to school every morning and pick her up every afternoon. Those were our special times. I'll never forget how she looked bounding down the hill toward the car, her fists full of papers, her hair backlighted by the afternoon sun.

Inspired by the example left us by our parents, Brenda and I determined to continue the holy heritage of family. In the winter we all went snowmobiling in the countryside and ice skating in the park. In the summer we hiked and picnicked in the mountains. In the fall we cut firewood, buoyed by the prospect of long winter evenings together in front of a roaring fire. We became "photography nuts," and we now have hundreds of pictures, and even more memories.

I will always be thankful I was free to be a father when Leah needed me most. Still, it was a choice. There were many things I could have done, but I chose to spend my time and energy being a husband and a father. What are you choosing?

In addition to time, children must have unconditional parental love if they are to grow up to be emotionally whole adults. In my work with professional groups, I frequently encounter men and women who overreact to the smallest slight, real or imagined. Others are defensive, while still others are withdrawn or have trouble relating to persons in authority. Again and again these difficulties have their roots in the parent-child relationship. As a general rule such people did not receive their parents' unconditional love when they were children. As a consequence, they are not emotionally whole persons.

Unconditional love is not dependent upon the child's performance. It is given freely, consistently. It enables a child to unconsciously separate his value as a person from his performance, good or bad. Unconditional love can be expressed in a variety of ways, but none is more effective than touching and telling. All children need to be held and hugged. They need to hear their parents say the three most powerful words in the human vocabulary — "I love you."

Almost four years ago, I was on my way to Anchorage, Alaska, and I finally had a few hours to myself. There were no phones to answer, no deadlines to meet, and no one scheduled for counseling. After a couple of hours I began to wind down, and as I did, I grew nostalgic, or philosophical, maybe both. Not being one to waste such feelings, I wrote my daughter a letter. I would like to share some of it with you:

"Dear Leah,

"It's been a while since I've told you what a special person you are. God has given you the gift of joy and self-confidence. I think you have tremendous people skills, and a real talent for public speaking and drama. When I was your age I was shy and introverted; my gifts were not developed at all. You are years ahead of me and I believe your accomplishments will far exceed my own. Never forget, though, that when God gives a person special gifts, He also gives them special responsibilities.

"I hope I've rubbed off on you these past fifteen years. I want you to catch the values which make my life rich. Here's a partial list of the things I hope you remember when you are grown and on your own.

"1. Attitude is everything — it can make or break you. It is the one thing no one can ever take from you — the freedom to choose how you are going to feel about a given situation. As the poet put it, 'Two men looked out through prison bars; one man saw the mud, one man saw the stars.'

"2. Relationships are the most important things in life. Do unto others as you would have them do unto you. Always be careful to use things and love people.

215

"3. Don't be afraid to fail. Nothing great was ever achieved on the first try. Learn from your failures and try again.

"4. God's will is not inhibiting. It frees you to fulfill your highest potential, while enjoying the most meaningful life possible.

"5. If you sin, God always stands ready to forgive. In fact, He is always more anxious to forgive us than we are to be forgiven.

"6. True joy is found in striving for God-given goals, even more than in obtaining them; so dare to dream big dreams, dare to attempt great things for God.

"That's enough for today. Let me close with some things I hope you remember when you are grown and gone. I hope you remember how crazy funny I can be when it's just the three of us and I'm letting my hair down. I hope you remember how much I love your mother and how special I think she is. I hope you remember how conscientious I was, how hard I worked, and how deeply I cared for people. Most of all I want you to remember how much I love God and how special you are to me. Never forget that I love you unconditionally. There is nothing you can do, no success or achievement, which will ever make me love you more. I love you, not because of what you do, but because of who you are.

"With all my love,

"Dad"

Boys need that kind of affirming love, too. Betsy Lee, in *Miracle in the Making,* writes: "My mother grew up in a family of girls. She was comfortable raising my sister and me, but my brother John confounded her from the day he was born.

"Distance loomed between Mom and John. She wasn't sure how to express her affection or tame his wild spirit. She seemed constantly to warn him of dangers.

"John frequently whined, 'You're always telling me that.'

"Mother always explained that her instructions were for his benefit. 'What do you think a mother is for?' she added.

" 'To love me,' he said.

"My mother was stunned, but prudent enough not to be defensive. She sought to change the way she communicated her love.

"My aunt, who had raised a son, told my mother, 'Boys aren't any different from girls. They need to be touched and kissed goodnight.' This came as a revelation to my mother, who thought cuddling would compromise her son's masculinity. But as soon as she started to demonstrate her love in direct, visible ways, John responded with greater warmth, and he began to respect her authority.

"As in all relationships, love had to be expressed in words and actions in order to grow."[4]

Some parents get the wrong impression when we talk of loving our children unconditionally. They mistakenly think that means they should never discipline their offspring. Nothing could be further from the truth. In fact, without proper discipline children will be unsure of their parents' love. When used appropriately, discipline is an act of love; it also creates a feeling of security by clearly defining the boundaries of behavior.

Discipline without love is tyrannical; it produces dependent people who are both hostile and fearful. Love without discipline is permissive; it trains children to be selfish and obnoxious. But when unconditional love and consistent discipline are both present in the family structure, they produce children who are emotionally healthy and well-adjusted.

"Dr. Stanley Coopersmith, associate professor of psychology, University of California, studied 1,738 normal middle-class boys and their families, beginning in the pre-adolescent period and following them through to young manhood. After identifying those boys having the highest self-esteem, he compared their homes and childhood influences with those having a lower sense of self-worth. He found three important characteristics which distinguished them:

"1. The high-esteem children clearly were more loved and appreciated at home than were the low-esteem boys.

"2. The high-esteem group came from homes where parents had been significantly more strict in their approach to discipline. By contrast, the parents of the low-esteem group had created insecurity and dependence by their permissiveness.

"3. The homes of the high-esteem group were also characterized by democracy and openness. Once the boundaries for behavior were established, there was freedom for individual personalities to grow and develop. The boys could express themselves without fear of ridicule, and the overall atmosphere was marked by acceptance and emotional safety."[5]

To fully satisfy the growing child's spiritual and emotional needs, the family must also provide spiritual training. While this should definitely include some form of graduated family devotions, designed with the child's needs in mind, in truth the most effective training grows out of real-life experiences. The most productive parents are those who watch for these special moments and make the most of them.

It has been called "striking while the iron is hot," a phrase which comes out of the old village blacksmith's shop. It refers to that precise moment when the metal has been heated to the exact temperature at which it is the most malleable. Life, too, has a way of creating situations like that in the experience of every child. Moments when circumstances have sensitized him to spiritual truths. The perceptive parent seizes those opportunities and, as a result, life-transforming truth is planted deep in the child's soul.

As this chapter draws to a close, I cannot help but think of those who have missed out on the gift of family. You may be one of these unfortunate people. Perhaps your parents divorced, or maybe you grew up in a foster home, or you may have been part of an abusive family. Whatever the case, you've probably lived your whole life with a gnawing ache, a deep emptiness. This chapter has perhaps identified that hurt for the first time. Now you realize that you are lonely for the family you never had. I wish there were some way to go back and make it up to you, but there isn't. Even now, as an adult, you feel that lack.

Don't despair. As hard as it may be to believe, the Bible declares that you are the object of God's special concern. Psalm 68:6 says, "God sets the lonely in families...." And He does — remember Sterling? That's the truest meaning of the Church — it's the family of God. It is truly a place to belong.

"You will do well to remember that.... You were aliens with no share in the divine nation of Israel. You were complete strangers to the covenants which contain the promise of God. You lived in a world without hope and without God. But because of your relationship with Christ Jesus the situation has changed. You who were far away have been brought near through the death of Christ.... So then, it follows that you are no longer foreigners and aliens; you are fellow-citizens with God's consecrated people, and members of the household [family] of God" (Eph. 2:12,13,19).[6]

Endnotes

[1]James Dobson, *What Wives Wish Their Husbands Knew About Women* (Wheaton: Tyndale House Publishers, Inc., 1975), p. 158.

[2]Ibid.

[3]Richard Exley, *Blue-Collar Christianity* (Tulsa: Honor Books, 1989), pp. 193,194.

[4]Reprinted by permission from *Miracle in the Making* by Betsy Lee, copyright © 1983, Augsburg Publishing House.

[5]James Dobson, *Hide and Seek, Self-Esteem for the Child* (Old Tappan: Fleming H. Revell, 1979), pp. 92,93.

[6]William Barclay, *The New Testament: A New Translation, Volume Two, The Letters and the Revelation* (London: Collins Publishers, 1969), p. 120.

Part IV

COMMUNITY

Unless we are particularly heroic or saintly persons, each of us needs a relationship with at least one other person who also seeks and trusts the simple way, the Simple Presence. Such a "spiritual friend" can be enormously supportive to us, and we to them. Even if you meet or write to each other only once a month, it can be enough. Just knowing that someone else is struggling for the simple way with you, whether or not you speak together often, is encouraging. You feel a little less alone, a little less tempted to fall mindlessly into complicating traps. Someone else is there who knows whether or not you are trying to pay attention to the simple way; that brings a kind of accountability that is important. When someone else knows and cares, then we pay that much more attention to what we're doing.

— Tilden H. Edwards

Part IV

COMMUNITY

We are complex beings, and our belonging needs can be met only through fellowship with God and a network of loving people. In relationship with God we satisfy our hearts' deepest hunger for spiritual intimacy. Through marriage and the family we have the opportunity to develop the kind of relationships which meet our inborn need for emotional intimacy. Yet, for all of that, there is still a longing for a place to belong, an extended family, a community of believers where we can know and be known.

The Church is supposed to meet our need for a place to belong, but too often it simply tends to be a reflection of our impersonal culture. Gone is the country church with three-generation friendships, all-day singings and dinners on the grounds. Now most of us worship in huge sanctuaries filled with strangers. The preaching is probably better, the ministry of the Spirit more obvious; yet, for all of that, our hearts still hunger for relationships.

In *All You Lonely People, All You Lovely People,* John Killinger writes: "Anne and I have lived in this city a little more than five years. In that time, we have not found a church where we really feel at home. We have attended many services of worship and talked to countless persons, always looking for something but never quite able to zero in on it. We joined one church soon after we came to town, but never achieved a feeling of really belonging there. . . .The people were friendly, in a polite sort of way, but it rarely went further than that. We never got over the feeling that we were outsiders."[1]

In response Bruce Larson has suggested: "The neighborhood bar is possibly the best counterfeit there is to the fellowship Christ wants to give his church. It's an imitation (to be sure), dispensing liquor instead of grace, escape rather than reality, but it is a permissive, accepting, and inclusive fellowship. It is unshockable. It is democratic. The bar flourishes not because most people are alcoholics, but because God has put into the human heart the desire to know and be known, to love and be loved, and so many seek a counterfeit at the price of a few beers."[2]

He goes on to say, ". . .a fellowship must exist where committed people can begin to be honest with one another and discover the dimensions of apostolic fellowship."[3]

That's quite an order, isn't it? A place to belong, a place to know and be known, a place to love and be loved. A place where we can experience apostolic fellowship rather than just talking about it.

Yet, such a thing must be possible, otherwise God would not have placed the desire for it in our hearts. And without it, life is dull and flat; without it, Christianity is only half a religion, reconciling us to God, but not to each other.

Yet, even as we hunger for true fellowship, we also resist it. We hang onto our independence with a stubborn tenacity. Robert L. Browning, Professor of Christian Education at Methodist Theological School in Ohio, says, "This profound need both for independence and belonging can be seen in every anthropological study and in all psychological analyses in one form or another."[4]

How well we balance these needs determines the veracity of our fellowship and our authenticity as individual persons. When we truly become part of a Biblical fellowship, we make ourselves available to the Body without forfeiting our individuality.

Several social factors also contribute to our inability to build deep and lasting fellowships. We are a mobile society. Jobs and career advancement make it necessary for us to move, often several times, especially during the early stages of our career. As a consequence, we are often separated from our roots, our family, our childhood friends. This trauma is especially hard on children. Not only are they separated from their extended family — grandparents, aunts, uncles and cousins — but they soon learn to build only superficial friendships in order to minimize the pain of leaving.

Additional factors include air-conditioning and television. Before the days of air-conditioning, the heat of summer forced people to spend evenings on the front porch.

It was simply too hot to stay indoors. The front porch became a gathering place, not only for the family itself, but for anyone who might pass by. Invitations to stop and chat, to have a glass of lemonade, were not uncommon. As air-conditioning became more and more the norm, it became simply too hot to spend the evening out of doors. So in time the front porch disappeared. And with its passing, so went the casual visit, the long evenings of friendly conversation.

Now consider the impact of television. With just the flick of a switch a person can have instant relationship, and without risk. Television brings "life" right into our living rooms. It's not "real," of course, and we experience it only vicariously, but once again we isolate ourselves from each other. Even family communications often fall prey to television's inane offerings as evenings and mealtimes are given over to the news and sitcoms. As a consequence, our communication skills deteriorate and we become strangers in our own homes.

These harsh realities were made frighteningly clear to me when Brenda's parents installed a satellite dish at Vallew, their retirement home in the country. By sharing this incident I certainly do not mean to cast them in a bad light, for they are exceptional people of unusual hospitality and extraordinary people skills. Still, this single event serves to illustrate an important point.

About ten years before retirement, Ben Roy purchased a piece of property in the country and built a small one-room cabin on it. We soon developed a family tradition of spending Thanksgiving there. Brenda's sister, her husband and their son, would join us. In a fit of holiday madness all eight of us would crowd into that one room, which served as kitchen, living room and bedroom. Not infrequently, both Leah and Scott would invite a friend to come along, bringing the total number of occupants to ten.

The overcrowding, and the inconvenience of sleeping on the floor, were far outweighed by the sense of family we enjoyed. The only source of heat was a small Ben Franklin-type stove which gave that noisy room a friendly feel. Our only entertainment was what we could provide for ourselves. Consequently, we spent the long evenings playing games, singing songs, and swapping family stories. As Leah grew older, she invited Todd, her future husband, to join us. And it was there that they learned about the Great Depression, about life in the 40s during the "Big War" with its shortages and ration cards, and about the courtship of Leah's grandparents.

Ben Roy is an early riser, and one of my favorite memories is of waking to the small sounds he made as he stirred up the morning fire, while the rest of us were still bedded down beneath our warm covers. Next he would brew coffee and bring me a steaming cup. Venturing an arm out from under my homemade quilt, I would manage to sip the scalding potion until I was fully awake. As the cabin warmed up, Ben Roy and I would sit there talking, sharing the quiet of the early morning while around us the rest of the family slept peacefully.

As retirement drew nearer, Ben Roy added a garage and two bedrooms to the cabin. After that when we came for Thanksgiving, it was much more convenient, but something special had been lost. About three years ago he retired and turned that cabin into a lovely three-bedroom home. It's beautiful, and the two full baths, plus the dishwasher and dining room, make staying there very comfortable. But I can't help but miss the family warmth generated when we all used to crowd into that one room.

The last vestiges of those special times disappeared when Ben Roy installed the satellite dish and the VCR. After our last Thanksgiving visit Leah said: "It doesn't seem like Vallew any more. All we do is watch television. We never sing, or play games, or just talk. We don't have any family time." How right she was. In those ten short years, we had experienced in microcosm the social change television had brought to America.

Of course, we are not going to reverse "progress," and we wouldn't want to. Still, we must recognize how these social factors have negatively affected our relationships, and then make the necessary adjustments to our lives. Gone are the social structures which once created an environment in which relationships could grow and develop naturally. Now we will have to make a special effort to cultivate a place of community in which people are afforded the opportunity of interacting with each other. And we will have to build on those interactions if we hope to experience the kind of relationships for which our hearts so desperately hunger.

At one time the local church provided that environment; unfortunately, now it seems only to add to this mounting frustration. Far too often its primary focus is on the weekly worship service and little else. Worshippers, desperate for real fellowship, come and are given little or no opportunity to interact with each other. The very structure of worship prohibits such interpersonal exchange. Its focus is celebration, not community.

Most churches are so large that it's easy to get lost in the crowd. And it doesn't take a congregation numbering two or three thousand either. Studies indicate that an individual can become personally acquainted with as many as 60 persons, but will tend to feel isolated in groups larger than that. If he doesn't see a familiar face, if no one remembers his name, he will feel left out no matter how vibrant the worship. If this happens week after week, it will undermine his personhood and he will begin to doubt his self-worth.

Over the past 10 or 15 years, concerned Christians have addressed these issues. They have encouraged more lay involvement through a variety of means including Body ministry and sermon dialogue. Many of these changes were superficial and temporary, but some of them have proven enormously effective. Yet, for all their good, they have done almost nothing to satisfy the hunger for true fellowship. In truth, the Church cannot solve its need for community by changing its style of celebration. That's like trying to cure one patient by treating another.

When we try to force the weekly worship service to accommodate celebration and community equally, we are engaging in an exercise in futility. Celebration and community are not rivals vying for equal time on Sunday morning; rather, they are complementary manifestations of the true Church. They are different in purpose, but equal in value. Celebration focuses primarily on God. It is the Church ministering to the Lord. As a consequence of the corporate worship experience, the individual believer's spiritual needs are met, but not his need for fellowship, his need to belong. Celebration may include community, but its primary focus is on worship rather than relationship.

The truth of the matter is that the weekly worship service cannot provide the quality of fellowship our hearts cry for, nor should it. Christian education classes, if they are so structured, can provide a measure of community, as can pot-luck dinners and church socials. Still, the depth of fellowship we seek will continue to elude us unless we consciously plan for it. It cannot be forced, but it can and must be cultivated. Hence the emergence of fellowship groups, usually consisting of 12 to 18 people each.

As we formulate our model for a fellowship group, let's return to Bruce Larson's "counterfeit" illustration. As we saw, he says, "The neighborhood bar is possibly the best counterfeit there is to the fellowship Christ wants to give his church."[5] Remember, he is talking about a "neighborhood bar" with a regular clientele who know and trust each other. These are not drunks or derelicts, but average people who are willing to buy a few beers, if only someone will listen to them without being critical or judgmental. Over a period of months, perhaps even years, they come to know each other — they form a kind of informal brotherhood. They don't "join," but they certainly belong.

Now apply that principle to the local church. First, it takes time to build relationships; therefore, a fellowship group should meet regularly, at least bi-weekly. The format should be structured, but informal. The emphasis must be on relationships, not teaching.

As the level of trust among participants develops, the sharing will become more personal and of greater substance. A sense of group identity will be formed. Individuals within the group will begin to build personal relationships. By living in relationship with each other, they will naturally come to feel a responsibility for one another and will begin to reach out to each other. They will get together for coffee, they will talk by phone, they will do little caring things for each other. They will celebrate birthdays together, remember anniversaries, form prayer partnerships — in short, they will "be there" for each other.

Fellowship groups are the relational heart of the local church, the core of New Testament fellowship, the answer to our social loneliness. They are an extended family providing community. They give us a place to know and be known, they make New Testament fellowship a reality — even in our busy, impersonal world.

Endnotes

[1]*All You Lonely People, All You Lovely People,* by John Killinger, copyright © 1973. Used by permission of Word Incorporated, Dallas, Texas, p. 11.

[2]Keith Miller and Bruce Larson, *The Edge of Adventure (Waco: Word Books, 1974),* p. 156.

[3]Ibid., p. 157.

[4]Robert L. Browning, "Belonging: A Sacramental Approach to Inclusion and Depth of Commitment," quoted in *Congregations: Their Power To Form and Transform,* edited by C. Ellis Nelson (Atlanta: John Knox Press, 1988), p. 177.

[5]Miller and Larson, p. 156.

Chapter 19

"AS IRON SHARPENS IRON"

Few things in life are more rewarding than true friendship. G. D. Prentice said, "A single real friend is a treasure worth more than gold or precious stones." A real friend is a person with whom, as Emerson said, "I may think out loud." With a true friend, I may share my secret dreams without fear of being put down, and even my fears without risk to the relationship.

A true friend hears you when you speak your heart. He supports you when you are struggling; he corrects you, gently and with love, when you are wrong; and he forgives you when you fail. Such a friend prods you to personal growth, stretches you to your full potential. And, most amazing of all, he celebrates your successes as if they were his own. As the wise man said so many centuries ago, "A friend loves at all times..." (Prov. 17:17), and:

"Two are better than one,
   because they have a good return for
      their work:
If one falls down,
   his friend can help him up.
But pity the man who falls
   and has no one to help him up!
Also, if two lie down together, they
      will keep warm.
   But how can one keep warm alone?
Though one may be overpowered,
   two can defend themselves.
A cord of three strands is not quickly
      broken."

Ecclesiastes 4:9-12

Yet, friendship is also a high-risk endeavor, and after we've had a few disappointing experiences we tend to be less inclined to reach out to others. *LEADERSHIP* editor Terry Muck observed: "Personal relationships seem to grow more complicated as the years go by. Most grade schoolers view their classmates as a pool of potential companions. They simply pick the ones they want to befriend and do it. It's like picking the ripest, juiciest apple from the orchard. It never occurs to children that there might be years when the apple tree won't bear a very good crop, or they might lose the capacity or desire to pick.

"The years teach differently. If surveys of American adults, particularly males, are any indication, friends become a rarer commodity as the years go by, more like gold than apples. Many of us are forced to treasure the few we have and become less optimistic, frighteningly skeptical about making new ones. It becomes a fearful process to bare bruised feelings and memories to strangers — the very process that establishes fellowship."[1]

The question before us, then, is not simply how to make friends at mid-life and beyond. But more precisely, how to build relationships that last. There's something special about a lifelong friendship, especially between brothers in the Lord. It becomes the standard by which all other friendships are measured. And we tend to think of such long-term friends as a team rather than simply as individuals. For instance, it's hard to think of David without Jonathan, Paul without Timothy, D. L. Moody without Ira Sankey, or Billy Graham without Cliff Barrows or George Beverly Shea.

The first characteristic of true friendship that comes to mind is compatibility, that personal "chemistry" which draws one person to another; but that's too simplistic. It may be an initial factor, but it takes more than chemistry to build a relationship which spans the years. Personal wholeness — the quality of character, the depth of integrity — may be closer to the truth.

It has been noted that unhealthy people cannot establish a healthy relationship. Nor can a whole relationship be built between wounded people. In short, a relationship is no better or stronger than the people involved in it. Persons who are unhappy, wounded or bitter find it almost impossible to maintain lasting relationships. Because of their past hurts and disappointments, they continually misinterpret and overreact.

Like friendship, life itself is a high-risk endeavor, and no one escapes unscathed. If the spiritual and emotional injuries received during the normal process of living are

BUILDING RELATIONSHIPS THAT LAST

not healed, they can become infected. In which case, they will alter one's perception of both people and events, while undermining his future relationships. If you have had a pattern of unsuccessful relationships over the years, it would be wise to examine your emotional wholeness in the presence of God.

Begin by asking the Lord to reveal any woundedness which might be in you. Be sensitive to the thoughts and impressions which come to mind. This is often how the Lord speaks to us. Be aware of what's going on inside of you — the feelings, the involuntary memories. As unresolved issues surface, offer them to the Lord for healing. If they are long-standing, and deeply rooted, you may need the help of a caring, qualified pastor or Christian counselor to find complete healing.

Not infrequently though, the breakdown in relationships lies with the other person. He is the one who is not whole. Those of us who are committed Christians have what I call a "good Samaritan complex." That is, we are extremely compassionate, and continually look for life's discards, those wounded souls who are in desperate need of a friend. That's a wonderful ministry, but if we confuse it with friendship, we are setting ourselves up for a real disappointment.

True friendship requires reciprocity. Both participants must get something from it. A relationship which consistently drains one member is bound to run dry sooner or later. In a genuine friendship, both participants give and receive. Without this balance no lasting friendship can be maintained. In fact, without a mutual giving and receiving, the relationship cannot be called a friendship at all.

Many so-called friendships perish right here. Compassionate people often fall prey to this kind of one-way relationship. They have an enormous need to minister to people, but they haven't learned how to relate to others as friends or peers. Consequently, they are often drained and lonely, even though they are constantly involved with countless people.

The other half of this frustrating relationship is the recipient of all this ministry. He tends to be insecure, with a long history of rejection. As soon as he is given a measure of attention, he fastens himself to the befriending person. Rather than developing a circle of friends, he tries to meet all of his belonging needs through this one individual. When the "minister" has nothing left to give, the relationship dies a slow death, and both parties end up frustrated and disillusioned. The recipient's perception of conditional friendship is reinforced, as well as his negative feelings about himself. The "minister," on the other hand, ends up feeling guilty and wondering why he can't seem to have a normal relationship with anyone.

Don't misunderstand me, I'm not suggesting that we ignore the friendless and those beaten down by the harsh vicissitudes of life. I'm simply stating that we need to clearly differentiate between ministry and friendship. Furthermore, those of us who are committed to befriending the lonely must make sure that we have other reciprocal relationships in which our belonging needs are nourished; otherwise, we will soon burn out.

In my work as a pastor, I have found it not only helpful but necessary to monitor my relationships to make sure I am maintaining an appropriate balance between ministry and friendship. I define ministry as those relationships from which I receive nothing but the satisfaction of knowing I have faithfully served my Lord and His hurting people. On the surface, such relationships may appear very much like friendships. They may include shared meals, long talks, even holidays spent together. But the truth is, in this kind of ministry relationship I am constantly giving of myself without receiving from it anything of eternal value.

As a shepherd, I am called to serve, to pour myself into the lives of God's people. Yet, even as I do this, I must be careful to make sure that I do not allow others to become overly dependent upon me. True ministry is designed to produce spiritually mature and emotionally whole individuals. To accomplish this goal, I insist that those to whom I minister take advantage of all the ministries afforded them by the church. If they consistently refuse to do so, I gently, but firmly, refuse to see them any longer. If I did not do so, I would develop a neurotic following who would eventually consume my life and ministry.

And in order to maintain my spiritual vitality, I must balance my ministry with nourishing friendships. These are reciprocal relationships in which each of us involved finds food for our souls. We exchange ideas, discuss the scriptures, joke together, and pray together — not as pastor and parishioner, but as friend with friend. This kind of relationship is what the writer of Proverbs described as iron sharpening iron. (Prov. 27:17.) Spiritual ministry does take place, but it is a consequence rather than an objective. And for a brief time I am free of that fearfully heavy burden of being "the man of God."

In building this kind of nourishing relationship, we must proceed with caution. How well I remember one of my early ventures. I moved far too quickly in attempting to establish a friendship and soon realized that, despite his protests to the contrary, my potential friend did not want his pastor to be "real." As soon as he discovered my "feet of clay," my human struggles, he lost all confidence in me. The resulting pain didn't go away for a long time.

Yet it is not only ministers who are at risk in transparent relationships, but all of us. Not infrequently we are our own worst enemies. With a boldness that often borders on insanity we plunge headlong into new relationships without ever testing the waters. Too late we discover that our trust was misplaced, that the treasures of our heart have been cast like so many pearls before swine. An experience or two like that and we are soon tempted to comfort ourselves with the bread of loneliness.

In order to maximize the benefits of friendship, while minimizing the risks, it is a good idea to proceed with circumspection. The wise man wrote, "A righteous man is cautious in friendship. . ." (Prov. 12:26). Jim Smith of Highland Park Presbyterian Church in Dallas recommends that to move beyond a mere superficial relationship, we be as bold as turtles. He says, "To move to something more intimate requires a careful testing of the other person over a long period of time."[2]

Give your potential friend a small piece of your heart. If he (or she) treats it with respect and understanding, or better yet, reciprocates, then share a little more of yourself. In this way, you can build a true friendship without risking your whole heart at once. Ultimately, the depth of your relationship will depend upon the degree to which you are willing to share your true self.

C. S. Lewis said, "Eros will have naked bodies; friendships naked personalities."[3] This simply means that in order to build a genuine relationship, we must be our real selves. No one can develop a friendship with an actor, that is, a person who always hides his true self behind a mask or facade. In that case, the person you see is just a figment of the imagination, a myth lacking substance and reality.

At the heart of a true friendship is real openness. I'm not talking about "psychological nudity" or the "tell-all" school of thought which characterized the early days of encounter groups. Rather, I'm talking about being ourselves, about being transparent, not just honest. That is risky, to be sure, but it is the only way to develop in-depth friendships. A relationship built on anything else is just a sham — a make-believe friendship between people who are pretending to be something other than who they really are.

Endnotes

[1]Terry C. Muck, "From the Editor," *LEADERSHIP*, Fall Quarter, 1984, p. 3.

[2]Paul D. Robbins, Jim Smith quoted in "Must Men Be Friendless?" *LEADERSHIP*, Fall Quarter, 1984, p. 27.

[3]Ibid., C. S. Lewis quoted p. 28.

Chapter 20

SPECIAL FRIENDS

An integral part of all lasting relationships is a genuine commitment. Whether we are talking about marriage or friendship, it is safe to say that sooner or later that relationship will be tested. It will have to weather some storms if it is going to stand the test of time. And without a genuine commitment, it will not long survive.

"Soon after Jack Benny died, George Burns, the quintessential song and dance man, was interviewed on a TV talk show. When asked about his relationship to Jack, George flicked his unlit cigar and answered with that distinctive voice so experienced in delivering punch lines. 'Well,' he said, 'Jack and I had a wonderful friendship for nearly fifty-five years; Jack never walked out on me when I sang a song, and I never walked out on him when he played the violin.' Though couched in jest, Burns expressed the fact of commitment. He and Benny were genuinely close friends — committed friends. While they were not given to a formal covenant, hardly a day went by when they didn't talk, at least by telephone. Each would have done anything for the other. People who knew them envied their commitment."[1]

Unfortunately, there are many people who seem incapable of making this kind of commitment. Or perhaps they are simply unwilling to invest so much of themselves. When the going gets rough, they find it easier to slide off sideways and begin a new relationship, rather than demand of themselves the growth necessary to revitalize their present relationship. By so doing, they end up with several shallow, short-term relationships rather than a single, truly meaningful friendship.

The tragedy of such a life is not simply that its relationships lack depth, but that it dooms one to live the same shallow cycles over and over again. Each new encounter follows a now familiar path. The same experiences are shared, the same stories told, the same feelings expressed. They may seem new, because there is a new audience to hear and appreciate them, but in the person's heart, he knows better. And its just a matter of time until he exhausts his superficial sharing, becomes bored with the relationship and begins looking around for someone new.

Every relationship goes through periods of testing, times of boredom, times when those involved in it must decide whether they are going to develop it to its fullest potential or slide off sideways and begin a new one. Developing a true friendship means digging deep. The stuff of which it is made comes from the depth of the soul. Those who dare to make the commitment discover not only the treasure of a true friend, but the truth about themselves. In digging deep, to bring fresh material to the relationship, they mine their own potential and expand the boundaries of both their relationship and the quality of their own lives.

M. Basil Pennington addresses this subject in *A Place Apart:* "The rigorous demands of true friendship, the gift of oneself, one's time, one's preferences, the nakedness and honesty, are beyond the price many are willing to pay — those who have not yet experienced what is purchased by such a price."[2] He then adds, *"Anyone who has been graced with true friendship knows the cost and knows the worth."*[3] (emphasis mine)

Another quality in all lasting relationships is honest communication. And real communication can only flourish in an environment of love and trust. A person must feel safe before he will open up and share his whole heart. Only when he knows that we will really listen to him can he risk the depth of disclosure that produces intimacy, which is the true measure of friendship.

In a *LEADERSHIP* article entitled "Must Men Be Friendless?" Paul D. Robbins writes: "All of us want a friend who will pick up our signal and listen. . . . To have someone who wants to absorb us, who wants to understand the shape and structure of our lives, who will listen for more than our words, is one of friendship's greatest gifts."[4]

Over the years I have worked hard to be a good listener, at least in part, because I so desperately need someone to listen to me. I think best out loud, with a trusted friend. If he will hear me out, without challenging me or feeling it necessary to give me advice or instruction, I will usually come to the right conclusion on my own. That is not to say that there will never be a time for hard questions, even confrontation, but only that we must grant our friend the chance to find his own way first. And often the most helpful thing we can do is accept him and listen with love as he thinks out loud.

Several years ago I was going through a difficult time. A number of factors combined to produce enormous stress. Brenda's mother was undergoing radiation treatment for an ovarian cancer. I had just been asked to resign from my position as associate pastor and was experiencing great difficulty in finding my place in the ministry. In desperation I sought the counsel of a friend and fellow pastor. It wasn't formal counseling; just one friend sharing with another.

I'm sure I made some rash statements as I ventilated my grief and anger. Under the circumstances my perceptions were undoubtedly clouded, yet Tex never corrected me or even advised me. He simply listened nonjugmentally and with love. Time after time I left his presence feeling encouraged and renewed. Not only did he help me through a difficult period in my life, he also taught me the meaning of friendship and the healing power of listening.

There are times when honest communication means we will have to confront. To leave our concerns and differences unspoken would not only betray our friend but undermine our friendship as well. Unresolved differences, even though they may seem insignificant, wear on us like a pebble in our shoe. If they are not dealt with, they will eventually erode the relationship. How we deal with them is of critical importance, however. Proverbs 12:18 declares, "Reckless words pierce like a sword, but the tongue of the wise brings healing."

Well do I remember, and with great pain, an incident I mishandled some years ago. It involved a young man I was disciplining in the Lord. He was terribly immature and had developed the habit of missing work. His irresponsibility became so bad that he was suspended. After much prayer, I interceded on his behalf, assuring his employers that if he were given another chance things would be different. He was reinstated, and things went fine for almost a month. Then one evening I dropped in to see a friend and the young man was there. I knew he was supposed to be working evenings, so I lost my temper. In the presence of others, I berated him. I told him that he had betrayed my confidence; that he had not only damaged his own reputation, but my good name as well. Once I got started, I couldn't seem to quit. Finally, he left; and, too late, I realized what I had done. I had destroyed him.

First, my timing was wrong. This was a private matter between him and me, and I had no business discussing it in public. Second, I attacked him personally. I failed to distinguish between his behavior, which was inappropriate, and his person. I made him feel stupid and irresponsible. I belittled him in front of our friends. Third, my attitude was all wrong. I wasn't really concerned about him, not at that moment. I was just plain mad. He had let me down. He had made me look foolish to his employers. My pride was hurt, and I was determined that he was going to pay!

A couple of days later I apologized, but it was too little too late, and our friendship never recovered. He lost his job and soon left town. I haven't heard from him in ten years, but I can't help wondering if he has ever recovered from the fearful tongue-lashing I gave him. I fear that I may have damaged his fragile self-image for life. He was wrong to miss work, but my sin against him was far greater.

For years thereafter I found it all but impossible to be confrontive in relationships lest I inflict another mortal wound. And in my reticence I allowed other friends to do great damage to themselves. Maybe my warnings would have fallen on deaf ears, maybe my friends would have resented the confrontation, maybe our friendships would have been affected; still, I had a responsibility to speak, and I didn't. My concerns were legitimate, but that in no way justifies my negligence.

These two extremes illustrate the most common ways we fail in our relationships. Either we speak too quickly or only after things have passed the point of no return, that is, if we speak at all. Either we speak harshly in anger, or we hold our peace out of fear or a misguided love. True friendship requires that we speak the truth in love. (Eph. 4:15.) Truth without love is harsh. Love without truth is permissive. But the truth spoken in love is redemptive!

Several weeks ago I was agonizing over a situation in which I had to discipline a man. Though I felt that I had done the right thing, and in the right way, I still grieved for him. As I was wrestling with my feelings in prayer, I sensed the Lord speaking to me and I wrote:
"My son,
power is a dangerous thing,
and it must always be mitigated
with My eternal love.
"I will cause you to feel
the pain of My discipline
even when it is toward another.

You will feel every sting
of the lash in your own flesh.
You must, or in your zealousness
you would go too far.
You will grieve,
even as Samuel grieved for Saul.

"Yet I will also make you feel
the awful pain of their sin,
for if you do not feel
that terrible pain,
you will draw back
from administering the discipline
of the Lord."

Confrontation is invariably necessary. A relationship seldom achieves its full potential without it; but it is almost always doomed to failure unless it grows out of a deep trust built on honest communication. Even then, it must be handled with sensitivity and tenderness. If our friend is not convinced of our genuine concern, he will likely become defensive and withdrawn. Therefore, it is extremely important to take great care to create a safe place, a place of affirmation and acceptance. A place where he can be assured, again and again, of our love. Even then confrontation will be risky and should be undertaken only after we have carefully prepared our hearts before the Lord.

Remember, the ultimate purpose of friendship is not accountability but nurture. True friends are committed to protecting each other, to be sure. You must protect me from myself, even as I protect you from yourself. Yet, if that becomes the primary function of the relationship, it will not long survive. *The bread which nourishes our soul is acceptance and communication, not accountability.*

Some years ago Bruce Larson, author of such best-sellers as *No Longer Strangers* and *The Relational Revolution*, returned to the pastorate after 21 years of writing and speaking about relationships. When he introduced himself to the University Presbyterian Church in Seattle, he said:

"Let me describe myself. I have an extraordinary measure of the gift of faith; I believe anything is possible with God. I also have a great gift of hope; I really believe tomorrow is going to be the dawn of the Christian era. But where I got shortchanged is in the area of love. I'm insecure, I'm touchy, I'm critical, I'm fault-finding — help me! I'm not a very good lover at all.

"That, incidentally, is why I write so much about love relationships — because I'm so poor at them. My life is strewn with broken and painful relationships. That's why I've become a specialist, I guess, in these things! I'm basically selfish, a hermit. Before I came here, I lived six years on an island in the Gulf of Mexico; that tells you who I am. I preach intimacy and community because I need it so badly."[5]

As I read that now, I am almost moved to tears, so deeply can I identify with him. I'm not very good at relationships either; and yet I hunger for them with all my heart. I need people who will know me and allow me to know them. And I need people who will love me and allow me to love them. Yet, if I am not careful I find myself withdrawing. I don't want to be hurt again, nor do I want to fail in yet another relationship. Inside this middle-aged man's body is a little boy still looking for a place to belong. And it's this loneliness, this hunger for fellowship, which

enables me to overcome my fearful timidity and risk yet
another try at relationships.

"Jesus,
I've been thinking a lot about friends lately.
Everybody is talking about relationships,
and really knowing each other,
but no one seems to do much about it.
Or everyone wants to have the same friend
    — that person who's up in front of the crowd
   or the gal with the toothpaste smile
     and the winsome personality.

"Hardly anyone seems willing
to build relationships with ordinary people.
You know,
    — the harried housewife with three pre-schoolers,
   the overweight, under-confident teenager,
    or the quiet guy on the edge of the crowd.

"Who was Your friend, Lord?

"I know You had a lot of acquaintances,
and the twelve who shared the ministry,
but who was Your friend?
I mean the one person
with whom You could let your hair down.
Where You didn't have to watch every word
or meet someone's unending expectations.
You know,
where did You go when You had to get away,
but You couldn't bear to be alone again?

"Was Lazarus that special friend for You, Lord?
I think maybe he was.
I started to pray,

'Give me a friend like that,'
but I thought better of it.
Instead I pray,
'Let me be a friend like that.' "
"Amen."

Endnotes

[1]Paul D. Robbins, Jim Smith quoted in "Must Men Be Friendless?" *LEADERSHIP*, Fall Quarter, 1984, C.S. Lewis is quoted. p. 29.

[2]M. Basil Pennington, *"A Place Apart,"* quoted in *Disciplines for the Inner Life* by Bob Benson and Michael W. Benson (Waco: Word Books, 1985), p. 104.

[3]Ibid.

[4]Robbins, p. 28.

[5]"None of Us Are Sinners Emeritus," an interview with Bruce Larson, *LEADERSHIP*, Fall Quarter, 1984, p. 15.

Chapter 21

OWNING OUR MISTAKES

Most of us can probably identify with Bruce Larson who wrote, "My life is strewn with broken and painful relationships."[1] And if not broken relationships, at least disappointing and unfulfilling ones. The truth of the matter is, we are just not very good at that sort of thing. Although our hearts hunger for it, we can't seem to get the knack of sustaining relationships. We keep hurting those we love and destroying the very thing that is nearest to our hearts.

And as we examine our lives, it is probably these relational failures which grieve us the most, especially as we grow older. They're a double-edged sword. The pain of our own failures, the shameful memory of friends we've let down, cuts us to the core. And on the other side there's the bittersweet betrayal by a trusted friend. Bittersweet because even in our anguish, even in our deep hurt, we cannot forget the special camaraderie we once shared.

Time and time again the story of mankind is rent with the sorrow of friendship betrayed. And those tragedies have produced some of history's most poignant moments. Hear the pained disbelief as Julius Caesar exclaims, *"Et tu, Brutae?"* ("And you, Brutus?") when he sees his dear friend among his assassins. Or Jesus when He says, ". . .'Judas, are you betraying the Son of Man with a kiss?'" (Luke 22:48). Then there's the painful commentary near the end of Paul's last letter, a single sentence which says it all: ". . .Demas hath forsaken me, having loved this present world. . ." (2 Tim. 4:10 KJV).

Who among us has not cried out in great anguish, at one time or another, like David of old who lamented:
"If an enemy were insulting me,
        I could endure it;
if a foe were raising himself against
                me,
        I could hide from him.
But it is you, a man like myself,
        my companion, my close friend,
with whom I once enjoyed sweet
                fellowship
        as we walked with the throng at the
                house of God."

                                Psalm 55:12-14

"Even my close friend, whom I trusted,
he who shared my bread,
has lifted up his heel against me."

                                Psalm 41:9

Yet, for all of our painful failures, our hearts still hunger for the reality of true fellowship. Indeed, we cannot live without it — exist maybe, but not really live. True

Biblical fellowship does not have to be a thing of the past. We can still bond with one another, develop the kind of interpersonal relationships in which we are both known and loved. But we can't just wait for it to happen. We can't force it, but we must encourage it.

First, we must get rid of our unrealistic expectations. There are no perfect people, not even Christians, and there is no place where fellowship just happens. We have to work at it all the days of our lives. And we can't expect true friendship to be without its conflicts either. Most people are very much like us — a strange mixture of dust and deity. Capable one minute of magnanimous acts of charity, and given to petty bickering the next.

Second, we need to take the initiative. That may mean joining a small group, inviting someone out for coffee, making a commitment of ourselves and God to build a deep relationship with at least one person outside of our immediate family. We will be the richer for it, and so will the other person. Dr. Paul Tournier believes that no one can develop freely in this world and find a full life without feeling understood by at least one person. If that principle is true, and I believe it is, then this kind of in-depth relationship is not only beneficial but mandatory.

True fellowship cannot long survive if the individuals within the group are not willing to own their mistakes and do what they can to make restitution. I am convinced that most people can forgive our failures if they can be assured that we recognize our mistakes and are taking steps to correct them. What they cannot forgive is our bland denial, our unwillingness to accept the responsibility for our behavior. This is true whether we are talking about personal friendship, family relations or the fellowship of believers.

Watergate will probably be remembered as one of the most infamous political scandals in the history of our nation. It was a tragic and unnecessary abuse of power, but it need not have become the destructive and devisive issue it did. As Gordon MacDonald points out, "If only Nixon had said he was sorry the country (or most of it) would have most likely forgiven him and let him get on with his presidency."[2] But when he insisted on covering up his part in the conspiracy, the country felt betrayed and lost confidence in his leadership. They no longer felt they could trust him. The same principle applies to our relationships, whether with members of our own family or in the fellowship of believers.

The first time Todd visited in our home, I made a terrible mistake and humiliated Leah. She had made us coffee and when she went to pour it she discovered that the handle on the coffee pot was too hot to hold barehanded. Instead of getting a potholder, she grabbed the handiest thing — a kitchen towel with a fringe on the ends. When she returned to the stove and picked up the coffee pot, the towel caught on fire. Screaming, she dropped both the burning towel and the pot of boiling coffee. Thankfully, she wasn't burned, but we did have quite a mess.

Here's where the story takes its most embarrassing turn. I lost control and berated Leah right there in front of Todd.

"Why can't you ever do anything right?" I demanded. "You know better than to use a fringed towel around the stove. You're lucky you didn't burn the house down."

Once I got started, I couldn't seem to quit. It only took a little of that kind of humiliating criticism to reduce Leah to tears, and she ran upstairs to her room.

Brenda gave me a look which clearly said she thought I was one of the most insensitive fathers in the whole world. Without a word she followed Leah upstairs. I risked a glance at Todd who now sat in the living room, uncomfortable, not knowing what to do. A discomfiting silence settled between us, and I went to the kitchen to clean up the mess. By the time I had finished, I knew what I had to do.

Excusing myself, I went upstairs to find Leah. When she heard me coming, she turned her face to the wall and tried to stifle her sobs. I sat down on the edge of her bed and put my hand on her trembling shoulder. When she seemed to cringe beneath my touch, I thought my heart would break. What had I done to my little girl?

An apology was a must, but I didn't know how to begin. I was tempted to explain my behavior, tempted to say something like: "I'm sorry I lost my temper, but you know better than to use a towel around the stove," or, "I'm sorry I spoke to you like that in front of Todd, but what you did was so uncalled for." Somehow I realized that wasn't an apology as much as it was an excuse. It still pointed the finger of blame at Leah.

Finally I managed to accept the full responsibility for my un-Christlike behavior. I told Leah that there was absolutely no excuse for what I had done. I asked her to forgive me, and I told her that if she would come back downstairs I would apologize to Todd as well. Of course, she did, and that tragic scene had a happy ending. But had

I been unwilling to own my mistake and make restitution for it, our relationship might have been ruptured for life.

This is just one of many times that I have "sinned" against those closest to me. I've spoken to Brenda, unkindly, in anger. I've been impatient with staff members, insensitive to the feelings of friends, and demanding with those under my authority. Over the years I've been defensive in church board meetings. I haven't always spoken my mind, but when something bothers me on the inside, my negative feelings seem to emanate through my pores. I'm sort of like the octopus which releases an ink-black secretion when it's threatened.

Yet for all of my relational "sins," I have a significant number of relationships which have stood the test of time. Why? The grace of God undoubtedly, plus the mercy of my friends and co-workers. They have been Christlike in their forgiveness. And if I have had any part in maintaining these relationships, it has been a result of my sincere efforts to honestly accept the responsibility for my mistakes and make restitution where I could.

In addition to providing the raw materials for healing a wounded relationship, our recognition and acknowledgment of our mistakes also gives God a chance to redeem them. When we allow the painful discomfort of a strained relationship to call us to prayer, and to the honest soul-searching such prayer demands, we move into a growth mode, into a position of humility and vulnerability in which God can do His holy work in us.

No so long ago, I was going through one of those times. In an attempt to sort out things, I turned, as is my custom, to my prayer journal. In it I wrote:

"Lord,
The last few days
have been exceedingly painful.
It started with a misunderstanding,
which in retrospect was mostly my fault,
then I used 'hell' in a sermon
and offended some of the finest people
a person could ever hope to know.
After twenty-one years in full-time ministry,
you would think I would know better.
I can't believe I did it.
I feel like such a klutz!

"In my pain and embarrassment
I'm tempted to defend myself,
to shift some of the blame to others.
Surely it takes more than one person
to have a misunderstanding.
Pity tempts me,
and in my mind I hear myself saying,
'Poor me, no one understands.
Can't they see that I'm only one man,
that I have limitations,
that there's only so much of me to give,
only so much I can do?'
I'm tempted to plead for understanding —

" 'Anyone who writes and preaches
as much as I do should be allowed
an inadvertent slip occasionally.
And why do they remember
one inappropriate phrase anyway?
What about all the helpful, healing things
You have helped me say?'

"Then I get hold of myself
and remember all the affirming
things people do and say —
notes expressing encouragement,
a hug and an affirming word,
a positive phone call
at just the right time.
Still the pain won't go away!

"Again I cry out to You.
'Why, Lord, do I hurt so?'
Slowly things begin to come into focus.
Misunderstanding between friends is painful,
criticism is never pleasant,
but this is more than that!
This pain is not from the hands of men,
it's God's doing.
He's chastening me, cleansing me,
conforming me to the image of His dear Son.
He's redeeming my mistakes,
making even the wrath of men to praise Him.

"With this new understanding
I now embrace my pain,
not masochistically,
but as submissive clay
beneath the skillful fingers
of the Master Potter.
It still hurts,
but now it is no longer pointless.
It's pain with a purpose,
redeemed by the tender hands
of a loving Heavenly Father.

"This knowledge doesn't
make my mistakes any less offensive,
to me or to others,
but it does give me hope.
I am changing —
        taking on more and more
of His holiness —
and it's this encouragement
which gives me the grace to go on."

Endnotes

[1]"None of Us Are Sinners Emeritus," an interview with Bruce Larson, *LEADERSHIP*, Fall Quarter, 1984, p. 15.

[2]Gordon MacDonald, *Rebuilding Your Broken World* (Nashville: Oliver Nelson, A Division of Thomas Nelson Publishers, 1988), p. 157.

Chapter 22

RESTORING BROKEN RELATIONSHIPS

Finally there's the ultimate act of love and friendship — *forgiveness!* Without this selfless act of mercy, no relationship can long survive. Because we are fallen people living in a fallen world, we are destined to "sin" against those we love the most, and, in turn, they are destined to "sin" against us as well. Sometimes we sin hastily, without thinking, in a moment of anger. Sometimes we sin thoughtlessly, never considering the ramifications of our behavior. Sometimes we sin selfishly, deliberately, because we are thinking only of ourselves. And, rarely, we sin cruelly, premeditatedly. The tragic truth is, sin is a part of our relationships and, therefore, so must be forgiveness.

With shameful honesty I must confess that I have sinned in some way, great or small, against virtually all the relationships of my life. That admission pains me more than you can know, and I wish it were not so, but it is. I've sinned against Brenda who is the gift of God to me, the last person in all the world against whom I would want to sin, the one person I love above all others. I have sinned against Leah, my only child, my own flesh and blood. I have sinned against my parents, the very people who gave me life, against the very ones who would lay down their lives for me. Must I continue? Must I tell you that I have sinned against every church I have served as pastor, against each church board with whom I have worked, against every friend who has ever trusted me with his or her heart? I must, for only then can you see how pervasive, how insidious, sin really is. Only then can you understand how desperately dependent we all are upon the holy gift of forgiveness.

No one understood the human heart and the human condition better than Jesus. When Peter came to Him and asked, ". . .'Lord, how many times shall I forgive my brother when he sins against Me? Up to seven times?'" (Matt. 18:21), "Jesus answered, 'I tell you, not seven times, but seventy-seven times'" (Matt. 18:22). Now if that seems like a lot to you, let me remind you that *The New International Version* has a footnote on that verse which reads, "Or *seventy times seven.*" Why would Jesus make such a big thing out of forgiveness? Because sin is such a big thing in our relationships. And sin cannot be undone, it can only be forgiven!

Unforgiveness gives birth to bitterness, and bitterness is a luxury which few people can long afford. It is not an isolated emotion directed toward one individual or one situation. It's an infection which spreads throughout the entire human psyche. It distorts the personality, colors one's perception of events and other people, and even affects how one perceives God. It's a thief, robbing life of its joy. Untreated, it will ravish an individual, leaving him old and empty, just a shell of his former self.

A spirit of bitterness toward another person may or may not hurt the person against whom it is directed, but it is certain to destroy the soul of the one who harbors it. I remember a scene from "Amos 'n Andy" which graphically illustrates this tragic truth. There was a big man who was always slapping Andy across the chest. Finally, Andy had had enough and he told Amos, "I'm gonna fix him. I've put a stick of dynamite in my vest pocket and the next time he slaps me, he's gonna get his hand blown clean off!" Unfortunately, Andy failed to consider one relevant fact. While the dynamite was blowing that man's hand off, it would also be blowing a hole in his own heart!

The dynamite of bitterness may indeed hurt the person against whom it is directed, but only at a terrible cost to the one who is so bitter.

Janet (not her real name) was a marvelously creative and talented woman, but a deeply disturbed one. When she came to see me, she was holding her fourth marriage together by her fingernails. She was the mother of seven children and only two of them were living at home. The two oldest boys were living with their father, her first husband. One son was away at college, a 17-year-old daughter was in a foster home, as was her 16-year-old brother. Janet's current husband was in jail, and she was at her wit's end.

I didn't have to see her very many times before I realized that she was an extremely bitter person, and with good cause, I might add. At the root of it all was a deep sense of animosity toward her father. According to her accounts, while she was growing up he had been a stern disciplinarian who had meted out severe punishment for the slightest offense. He was a perfectionist, quick to criticize, but incapable of expressing love or affirmation.

Janet remembered being frequently sent to bed without dinner because of minor mistakes in her table manners. On other occasions her father had punished her with severe whippings, and occasionally he had held her head under water until she thought she was going to drown. Never could she remember having been hugged by her father or hearing him say that he loved her.

Consequently, as a small child she had felt rejected and hurt. Growing older, her hurt had turned into anger and then resentment. Now these many years later, it was full blown bitterness, and affecting every relationship in her life, even her relationship with God. Or maybe I should say, *especially* her relationship with God.

She had known the terrible satisfaction of "getting even" with her father. For years she had refused to see him and had cut off all communications. She had married against his will and moved a thousand miles away. By the time she came to see me, her bitterness had destroyed three marriages, seven children, and her sanity!

You may be tempted to argue that Janet had a right to be bitter, that her father was a mean and cruel man. I will grant you that, but it does nothing to change the tragic truth concerning the self-destructive nature of unforgiveness. It always destroys the one who harbors it!

Then there's Sally (not her real name), whose husband repeatedly disappointed her. He made some important decisions without consulting her, and that hurt. A major cross-country move followed, and hard on the heels of that came a series of business failures and a major financial crisis. Like Janet, her hurt turned into anger, then resentment, and ultimately into bitterness. A more sensitive man might have noticed her poorly disguised hurt, but Tom (not his real name) was not a sensitive man, so her adultery caught him by surprise.

She had tried to talk to him, tried to reason with him, but he wouldn't listen. He expected absolute trust and unconditional loyalty. She had tried to be the kind of wife he expected, but as one bad decision followed another she began to lose respect for him and to harbor resentment against him. At first, she was able to hide her hurt, but as her bitterness grew, it became more and more difficult to suppress. She lost all interest in sex, then in their home, and finally in God.

To make ends meet, she took a job working evenings so Tom could stay with the children. Soon her work became the focal point of her life, and finally she became involved with a series of other men. Once again, unforgiveness exacted its terrible toll. Sally knew the satisfaction of making Tom pay for his mistakes and failures, but at a price no one could afford.

Webster's New World Dictionary defines *bitterness* as "strong feelings of hatred, resentment, cynicism, etc." I'm sure that's accurate enough, but I think bitterness can best be defined simply as unforgiveness. If unforgiveness is not bitterness, it's certainly the seed which gives birth to it.

265

One of the real difficulties in dealing with unforgiveness is getting people to realize that they need to forgive. I remember a man who came to see me several years ago. He spent the entire hour recounting, with strong feelings, a long list of past hurts. At the end of the hour when I gently suggested that he might need to deal with his bitterness, he became quite indignant and assured me that he harbored no ill feelings. If his assessment had been true, if he had really forgiven those past hurts, he would not have felt the need to share them, nor would there have been such intensity in his accounts.

If you cannot talk about past hurts and betrayals without experiencing strong emotions, then you are probably still dealing with unforgiveness. Another dead giveaway is the way a person reacts to a given situation. For instance, I remember a man who once lambasted me in the church foyer, just before the service, simply because I had typed up a recommendation differently from the way he remembered it. His emotional response was totally out of proportion to the significance of the slight, whether real or imagined. Once I recovered from the initial shock, I realized that this incident was rooted in some repressed anger or bitterness. If you find yourself constantly over-reacting, then you too may be harboring unforgiveness.

Perhaps you're thinking that I don't need to tell you about unforgiveness and the bitterness that follows. You know all about it. You've been living with it for years. What you want to know is what you can do about it. How can you get rid of it? There's only one cure, and it's not easy; there's only one way to restore the relationship — forgiveness!

The feelings of forgiveness almost never precede the actual act. You must, by an act of your will, pronounce forgiveness; only then can you expect the desired emotions. Even then the emotions may not be fully experienced for some time. In truth, forgiveness is a choice, a spiritual discipline, rather than a feeling. If you wait for the supposed emotional motivation, you will quite probably spend much of your life in a self-made prison. Learn to act out your forgiveness, and you will discover a life of joy and freedom.

In *The Hiding Place,* Corrie ten Boom shares a personal experience which serves as a case in point: "It was at a church in Munich that I saw him, the former S.S. man who had stood guard at the shower room door in the processing center at Ravensbruck. He was the first of our actual jailers that I had seen since that time. And suddenly it was all there — the roomful of mocking men, the heaps of clothing, Betsie's pain-blanched face.

"He came up to me as the church was emptying, beaming and bowing. 'How grateful I am for your message, Fraulein,' he said. 'To think that, as you say, He has washed my sins away!'

"His hand was thrust out to shake mine. And I, who had preached so often to the people in Bloemindaal the need to forgive, kept my hand at my side.

"Even as the angry vengeful thoughts boiled through me, I saw the sin of them. Jesus Christ had died for this man; was I going to ask for more? Lord Jesus, I prayed, forgive me and help me to forgive him.

"I tried to smile, I struggled to raise my hand. I could not. I felt nothing, not the slightest spark of warmth, or charity. And so again I breathed a silent prayer. Jesus, I cannot forgive him. Give me Your forgiveness.

"As I took his hand the most incredible thing happened. From my shoulder along my arm and through my hand a current seemed to pass from me to him, while into my heart sprang a love for this stranger that almost overwhelmed me."[1]

Unfortunately, few people have the spiritual maturity or the depth of commitment to respond as she did. Instead, they harbor their hurts and imprison themselves in the pain of past injustices. And, as a consequence, they doom their most important relationships.

As you may suspect, unforgiveness is frequently the focal point of my counseling. And over the years I have discovered three simple steps which seem to facilitate forgiveness. If you are suffering from bitterness, I strongly suggest that you take these steps:

First, honestly confess your feelings. Many people, especially Christians, tend to deny their feelings when they are painful or if they seem somehow unacceptable. Of course, there can be no act of forgiveness until such feelings are frankly acknowledged and the need to forgive faced up to.

Second, acknowledge that you are powerless to change what you feel, and then give God permission to change your feelings. Ask Him to help you love with His holy love the person who has hurt you. Then release the offending party. Let go of every hurt, every desire for revenge, every thought of getting even or making the other person pay.

Many people have real difficulty at this point. They are afraid that if they do not punish the offending party, no one will. They are truly afraid to give God permission to change their feelings, because they fear that He will do just that, and they are not yet ready to take that step. But we cannot afford to wait until we are "ready." Life is too short. We must simply "choose" to let God change us just as we chose to pronounce forgiveness.

Third, in prayer specifically forgive each person who has injured you. For example: "God, I forgive (name) for humiliating me." "Lord, I forgive (name) for lying about me." "Father, I forgive (name) for. . . ." Continue in this manner until every remembered offense has been dealt with. You were not sinned against generally, but specifically, and so you must forgive specifically.

Many times in counseling, after leading people to utilize this simple three-step approach, I have witnessed personal transformations which can only be called miraculous. The persons enter my office bitter and disillusioned, weighed down with grudges, some which they have carried for years. An hour later, they leave, free from anger and alive to life and God.

I do not mean to suggest that this is an instantaneous once-and-for-all cure-all, but I am offering it as a strategy for handling bitterness and as a workable way of practicing forgiveness. These steps (which are really a form of prayer), like all prayer, open us to the resources of God. They give Him a chance to express His forgiveness through us, which in turn brings healing to the relationship.

The most important relationships of my life continue intact to this day only through the miracle of forgiveness. My father and I are close only because he forgave me time and again for my "smart mouth," my quick temper and my disobedience. My mother and I have a similar closeness and for the same reason. She, too, practiced the holy art of forgiveness. Brenda has forgiven me more times than I can count. Leah, too. And the special friends who have stood the test of time have all been generous in forgiving my relational failures. And I too have learned to practice the holy art of forgiveness, howbeit, not nearly to the degree I would like. In so doing I have been given the best of all gifts — a friend restored.

Few things in life are more painful than a broken relationship. If you've lived for any length of time, I need say nothing more. It is a universal pain. An inevitable consequence of our fallen condition.

Yet, by the same token, there is nothing, absolutely nothing, which can compare with the unspeakable gift of forgiveness! To know the healing power it works on a broken heart is joy indeed! A joy whose bliss surpasses, in intensity, even the pain of friendship betrayed. It restores that which was lost. It heals that which was wounded unto death. It is the act of God, through us, breathing the breath of life into that which was dead. It is the kiss of God which makes all things new!

Of this experience Walter Wangerin, Jr., writes: "One day Thanne stood in the doorway of my study, looking at me. I turned in my chair and saw that she was not angry. Small Thanne, delicate, diminutive Thanne, she was not glaring but gazing at me with gentle, questioning eyes. This was totally unexpected, both her presence and her expression. There was no reason why she should be standing there, no detail I've forgotten to tell you. Yet, for a full minute we looked at one another; and then she walked to my side where I sat. She touched my shoulder. She said, 'Wally, will you hug me?'

"I leaped from my chair. I wrapped her all around in two arms and squeezed my wife, my wife, so deeply in my body — and we both burst into tears.

"Would I hug her? Oh, but the better question was, would she let me hug her? And she did.

"Dear Lord Jesus, where did this come from, this sudden, unnatural, undeserved willingness to let me touch her, hug her, love her? Not from me! I was her ruination. Not from her, because I had killed that part of her. From You!

"How often had we hugged before? I couldn't count the times. How good had those hugs been? I couldn't measure the goodness. But *this* hug — don't you know, it was my salvation, different from any other and more remarkable because this is the hug I should never have had. *That* is forgiveness! The law was gone. Rights were abandoned. Mercy took their place. We were married again. And it was You, Christ Jesus, in my arms — within my graceful Thanne. One single, common hug, and we were alive again."[2]

The miracle of forgiveness does not change the past, nothing can; nobody can go back and undo the wrongs that we have suffered, the pain we have inflicted. But it does something far greater — it redeems the present, and it unlocks the future. When I forgive my friend his sin, I release him to know once again the blessedness of our relationship. When he forgives me, I too, experience new life. All is not lost. I have not ruined everything — wounded it, yes; but forgiveness has given me a second chance. This time I will do better. I will share more deeply, trust more completely, so help me God! Together we will drink deeply of the cup of forgiveness and love again!

Forgiveness will build a relationship that lasts!

Endnotes

[1]Corrie ten Boom with John and Elizabeth Sherrill, *The Hiding Place* (Chosen Books, c/o Fleming H. Revell, Old Tappan, NJ, 1971), p. 215.

[2]Walter Wangerin, Jr., *As For Me and My House* (Nashville: Thomas Nelson, 1987), pp. 90,91.

BIBLE REFERENCES

BIBLIOGRAPHY

Alexander, John W., ed. *Confessing Christ as Lord: The Urbana '81 Compendium.* Downer's Grove: InterVarsity Press, 1982.

Allen, R. Earl. *Bible Paradoxes.* Westwood: Fleming H. Revell.

Barclay, William. *The Beatitudes and The Lord's Prayer for Everyman.* New York: Harper & Row Publishers, Inc., 1968.

Barclay, William. *The New Testament: A New Translation, Volume II, The Letters & The Revelation.* Copyright © by William Barclay 1968, 1969. Published in Great Britain by William Collins Sons & Co. Ltd., and the U.S.A. by the Westminster Press. Used by permission.

Benson, Bob, and Benson, Michael W. *Disciplines for the Inner Life.* Waco: Word Books, 1985.

Christianity Today. "A Talk with the MacDonalds." 10 July, 1987.

Colson, Charles W. *Loving God.* Grand Rapids: A Judith Markham Book, Zondervan Publishing House, 1983.

Congregations: Their Power To Form and Transform, edited by C. Ellis Nelson. Atlanta: John Knox Press, 1988.

Dobson, James. *Dr. Dobson Answers Your Questions.* Wheaton: Tyndale House, 1982.

Dobson, James. *Hide and Seek, Self-Image for the Child.* Old Tappan: Fleming H. Revell, 1979.

Dobson, James. *What Wives Wish Their Husbands Knew About Women.* Wheaton: Tyndale House, 1975.

Ellison, Craig. W. "Loneliness: A Social-Developmental Anaysis," *Journal of Psychology and Theology,* 6:3-17, 1978.

Exley, Richard. *Blue-Collar Christianity.* Tulsa: Honor Books, 1989.

Exley, Richard, *Notes to Leah.* (unpublished).

Exley, Richard. *Perils of Power.* Tulsa: Honor Books, 1988.

Forward, Susan and Buck, Craig. *Betrayal of Innocence.* Los Angeles: Jeremy P. Tarcher, Inc., 1978.

Foster, Richard. *Money, Sex & Power.* San Francisco: Harper & Row Publishers, Inc., 1985.

Gilbert, Jim. "Superstar." Tulsa: Spirit & Soul Publishing Co., ASCAP, 1982.

Gordon, Arthur. *A Touch of Wonder.* Old Tappan: Fleming H. Revell, 1974.

Gordon, Suzanne. *Lonely in America.* New York: Simon and Schuster, 1976.

Hamilton, J. Wallace. *Where Now Is Thy God?* Old Tappan: Fleming H. Revell, 1969.

Hembree, Charles. *Pocket of Pebbles.* Grand Rapids: Baker Book House, 1969.

Herwaldt, Frederick, Jr. "The Ideal Relationship and Other Myths About Marriage." *Christianity Today,* 9 April, 1982.

Hobe, Phyllis, ed. *Dawnings.* Waco: Word Books, 1981.

Hunter, Gordon C. *When the Walls Come Tumblin' Down.* Waco: Word Books, 1970.

Joy, Donald M., Ph.D. *Bonding: Relationships in the Image of God.* Dallas, Word Incorporated, 1985.

Keyes, Ralph. *We the Lonely People.* New York: Harper & Row Publishers, Inc., 1973.

Killinger, John. *All You Lonely People, All You Lovely People.* Dallas: Word Incorporated, 1973.

Killinger, John. *For God's Sake, Be Human.* Waco: Word Books, 1970.

Kole, K.C. "Playing Together: From Couples That Play." *Psychology Today,* February 1982.

LEADERSHIP. "None of Us Are Sinners Emeritus," an interview with Bruce Larson. Fall Quarter, 1984.

Lee, Betsy. *Miracle in the Making.* Minneapolis: Augsburg Publishing House, 1983.

L'Engle, Madeleine. *Walking on Water.* Wheaton: Harold Shaw Publishers, 1980.

MacDonald, Gordon. *Rebuilding Your Broken World.* Nashville: Oliver Nelson, A Division of Thomas Nelson Publishers, 1988.

Mace, David R. *Love and Anger in Marriage.* Grand Rapids: Zondervan Publishing House, 1982.

Massey, Craig. "Why Don't You Talk To Me?" *Moody.* June 1982.

May, Rollo. *The Art of Counseling. New York: Abington —Cokesbury Press, 1939.*

Merton, Thomas. No Man Is an Island. New York: Harcourt Brace and World, Inc., 1955.

Miller, Keith. *Habitation of Dragons.* Waco: Word Books, 1970.

Miller, Keith, and Larson, Bruce. *Living the Adventure.* Waco: Word Books, 1975.

Miller, Keith, and Larson, Bruce. *The Edge of Adventure.* Waco: Word Books, 1974.

Morris, Desmond. *Intimate Behavior.* New York: Random House, 1971.

Muck, Terry C. "From the Editor." *LEADERSHIP.* Fall Quarter, 1984.

"None of Us Are Sinners Emeritus," an interview with Bruce Larson. *LEADERSHIP*, Fall Quarter, 1984.

Nouwen, Henri J. M. *Reaching Out.* Garden City: Doubleday, 1975.

Ogilvie, Lloyd J. *The Communicator's Commentary, Volume V: Acts.* Waco: Word Books, 1983.

Osborne, Cecil G. *The Art of Becoming a Whole Person.* Dallas: Word Incorporated, 1978.

Potok, Chaim. *The Chosen.* Copyright © 1967 by Chaim Potok. Reprinted by permission of The William Morris Agency, Inc.

Robbins, Paul D. "Must Men Be Friendless?" *LEADERSHIP,* Fall Quarter, 1984.

Rutledge, Aaron. *Pre-marital Counseling.* Cambridge, Massachusetts: Schenkman, 1966.

Ryan, John K., translator. *The Confessions of St. Augustine.* New York: Doubleday, 1960.

Samuel, Dorothy T. *Fun and Games in Marriage.* Waco: Word Books, 1973.

Stanton, Peggy. *The Daniel Dilemma.* Dallas: Word Incorporated, 1978.

Stewart, James S. *The Wind of the Spirit.* Nashville: Abingdon Press, 1968.

Swindoll, Charles R. *Growing Wise In Family Life.* Portland: Multnomah Press, 1988.

Tapestries of Life. Philadelphia: A. J. Holman Company, A Division of J. B. Lippencott Company, 1974.

ten Boom, Corrie, with John and Elizabeth Sherrill. *The Hiding Place.* Old Tappan: Chosen Books, Fleming H. Revell, 1971.

Thatcher, Floyd W., ed. *The Splendor of Easter.* Waco: Word Books, 1972.

Tournier, Paul. *The Violence Within,* translated by Edwin Hudson. San Francisco: Harper & Row Publishers, Inc., 1978.

Tournier, Paul. *To Understand Each Other,* translated by John S. Gilmour. Richmond: John Knox Press, 1962.

Valkins, Phyllis. "A Kiss For Kate." *Reader's Digest.* August 1982. Originally published in *The Denver Post.*

Wangerin, Walter, Jr. *As For Me and My House.* Nashville: Thomas Nelson, 1987.

Wangerin, Walter, Jr. *Ragman and Other Cries of Faith.* San Francisco: Harper & Row Publishers, Inc., 1984.

Whyte, Alexander, D.D. *Bible Characters.* Grand Rapids: Zondervan Publishing House. 1967.

Wood, Robert. *A Thirty-day Experiment In Prayer.* Nashville: The Upper Room, 1978.

Wright, Frank. *Pastoral Care for Lay People.* London: SCM Press LTD, 1982.

OTHER BOOKS BY RICHARD EXLEY

*Abortion
Pro-Life by Conviction
Pro-Choice by Default*

Blue-Collar Christianity

Perils of Power

The Rhythm of Life

The Painted Parable

*The Other God —
Seeing God as He Really Is*

**Available from
your local bookstore
or by writing:**

P. O. Box 55388
Tulsa, OK 74155-1388

Richard Exley is an intense person who cares deeply for people which is reflected in both his writing and teaching. He is widely recognized for his daily radio broadcast "Straight From the Heart" which focuses on people rather than issues and is touching America with the love of God.

Richard Exley is the author of five books: *Blue-Collar Christianity, Perils of Power, The Rhythm of Life, The Other God — Seeing God as He Really Is,* and *The Painted Parable.* He currently pastors Christian Chapel in Tulsa, Oklahoma, where he lives with his wife, Brenda.

To contact Richard Exley, write:

Richard Exley
7807 E. 76th St.
Tulsa, OK 74133-3648